AF552625

KENTUCKY'S CLARK

With

Bill Cunningham

Library of Congress Catalog Card Number: 86-061921
International Standard Book Number: 0-913383-06-6

Cover design and illustration by James Asher
Senior Executive Editor, Carol Asher
Back cover photograph by Mark Marraccini
Manufactured in the United States of America

All book order correspondence should be addressed to:
McClanahan Publishing House, Incorporated
Rt. 2, Box 32
Kuttawa, Ky. 42055
(502) 388-9388

DEDICATION

This work is dedicated to all Kentuckians who served in Vietnam, especially to those who died and were wounded there.

"And when the green of our graves has mouldered away, some gray warrior sitting by night at the blazing fire will tell thy deeds to his sons, and they shall bless and admire the men of old." William Lewis Lockwood

NOTE

The portions of this book in quotes and primarily used as introductory material at the beginning of each section, are excerpts from various works of Thomas D. Clark.

Bill Cunningham

A LINGERING FRONTIER

"**This was my early world.** Born alongside the road which Andrew Jackson's muddy Tennessee volunteers hacked and blazed diagonally across Mississippi to reach New Orleans in the fall of 1814 and in the heart of the Choctaw country, I grew up on a lingering frontier. Our house was a big old dogtrot log structure built by my pioneering great-grandfather, who followed the opening of cotton lands westward from Virginia and South Carolina. Here I lived, in fact, on two frontiers. One was the great landed sea of virgin soil and timber which had been wrested from the Choctaws by Andrew Jackson and General John Coffee in the Dancing Rabbit Treaty of September 27, 1830. There still remained after the great removal a healthy seed stock of Choctaws who proceeded to repopulate the land in the upper Pearl River country. My other frontier was that of cotton and timber. My people had come to the Mississippi country to grow cotton and had remained through the vast timber harvest of this century.

One could not stand by and see the great virginal yellow pine sentinels come tumbling down to let the sunshine strike the ground in the scope of their limb spread for the first time in a century and a half, without some emotional reaction. What had been a great canopy on the horizon in the morning was left a gaping hole on the land by evening, and the whole blue line of the horizon was itself reshaped."

Thomas D. Clark is a Kentucky landmark.

Born July 14, 1903, his life has fallen full breadth across this century.

His has been a time of the most drastic, and shocking cultural and social changes in the annals of mankind.

He himself has plowed behind a mule, spoken with the soldiers of Lee and Forrest as well as with former slaves. He has flown about the world and watched men walk on the moon--all of this in one broad sweeping lifetime.

All of this and much more.

Dr. Thomas D. Clark is not only a highly erudite and distinguished individual. He represents a uniquely resilient and historic American generation. Born in this century on the tails of reconstruction, his has witnessed two world wars and the emergence of this country as the strongest nation on earth.

The experiences of this age group have included the revolutionizing trauma of the Great Depression, racial upheaval, divisive wars and monumental political scandals such as Teapot Dome and Watergate.

A great number of Thomas Clark's compatriots have moved through all of these with great physical hardship and in many cases, extreme deprivations.

Yet they have not only survived, but thrived in helping to build the great middle class of this country.

To be sure, Tom Clark's generation has had its flaws. But as observers of change, it has no historical peers.

When any octogenarian speaks, it usually pays to listen.

But a conversation with Dr. Thomas Clark is especially informative. For in addition to his many years of life, he bears also impressive credentials of learning.

Clark came out of spirited and enlightened stock.

His maternal grandfather, Dionysius Clark Bennett, carried both the classical name and mind. Tom's mother Sallie was both a school teacher and mother of seven--an extraordinary feat in any age. She wielded tremendous intellectual influence over Thomas, who was the eldest, and the rest of the brood, instilling in them a love both of books and learning. "When my children were babies," Mrs. Sallie Clark once wrote, "I never rocked or sang to them to get them to sleep. I would take them in my arms and, because I liked to read very much, I always had a paper or book in reach. Perhaps they did not understand what I was reading aloud to them, but soon they would get quiet and go to sleep. T. D. would come to listen to my reading. Before he could read he could tell all about Columbus, Washington, Lee, Jackson, Grant, and many others."

Tom's father, John Collingsworth Clark--"Johnnie C." to his neighbors--was a hard working farmer. His family arrived in the Mid-South by way of Virginia and South Carolina. After Andrew Jackson and company had wrested much of Mississippi's current land mass away from the Choctaw Indians by way of the Dancing Rabbit Treaty of 1830, good cotton land was obtained by the Clark clan.

Thus by the late 1830's the Clarks and Bennetts were enmeshed in the northern Mississippi frontier farm life.

In the league of hard knocks and bumped heads, Tom Clark knew his beginning. He was born and reared on a cotton farm near Louisville, Mississippi, where the scars of reconstruction were still tender, and Confederate veterans met and commiserated.

By 1911 the notorious boll weevil had made its disasterous sweep across the South's cotton fields. Even now Clark still reflects upon those boyhood days. "...I found the first weevil in a cotton bloom on our farm. If I had been a fortune teller reading tea leaves, I could not have looked at a clearer omen of the future."

The future was one of stoic desperation, and finally defeat, for the cotton farmers of the Old South. Tom Clark and his family lived through it all, including the final abdication of King Cotton. That's why when he talks of the current plight of tobacco in Kentucky--people listen.

On the heels of the boll weevil came the cattle fever tick out of Texas into Clark's home community. It decimated the cattle of this northern Mississippi rural area. It was estimated that the tick alone cost the south between fifty and one hundred million dollars annually. And that was in valuable Union green and not the fading Confederate money wasting away in attics and cellars.

Finally, and perhaps most devastating, was the recurring attacks upon human life by insidious diseases. Malaria, tuberculosis, hookworm and pellagra laid waste the lean and work worn country folk of the South. In 1915, an estimated 2,490 persons died in Mississippi alone from tuberculosis.

It was a colorful if desperate time and place. Hardships abounded, but so did the former soldiers of Lee, Forrest and Jackson. Ex-slaves and Choctaw Indians also shared their growing up grounds with Thomas Clark.

All of this was part of young Tom's awareness when he humbly began his illustrious academic career in a little country school yard on a hot dusty road not far from his home.

Young Tom's advancement with his formal education was repeatedly interrupted by less pedantic, but broadening distractions.

After completing the seventh grade in the spring of 1915, he worked full time on the farm for two years. He assisted his father in growing cotton, sugar cane, peanuts and corn.

World War I broke upon the scene and found the eldest son of Johnnie C. too young for soldiery service, but just right for rigorous labors at the sawmill about a mile from his home.

It was during these logging days that the 15 year old youth developed a life-long love and appreciation for the forest. The timberline became embedded upon his conscience as a reminder of man's critical partnership with the land. The abuse of our natural resources and the need for their replenishment would become a personal passion for Thomas Clark the historian. Much later as a timber man himself he would write, "In this area I have not only an academic interest, but a vital active interest as a tree farmer attempting to correct the sins of the past by putting the land back to its original state of my boyhood."

Then, on his 16th birthday, Tom Clark embarked upon a new venture which would enhance further his love affair with earth's bountiful resources. He began his service as a cabin boy and deckhand on a dredge boat which was engaged in cutting a channel through the nearby Tallahega Swamp at the head of the Pearl River.

The lure of the river tempted Clark to pursue it as a

career. But an old riverboat captain from Paducah, Kentucky, H. L. Lewis, convinced him that there was not a very bright future in that type of work.

In 1921 the future historian enrolled in the Choctaw County Agricultural High School. Hewing and hauling crossties in the summer--terribly strenuous work--and applying himself to the books conscientiously in the winter, Clark was able to go home in the summer of 1925 with his high school diploma.

By the grace of a lucrative cotton harvest that fall from ten acres of land his father had given him, he had sufficient funds to enroll at the University of Mississippi at Oxford. There he excelled as a student and developed his skills as a writer and debater.

During the humid summer vacation months of 1926 and 1927, Clark worked once again upon the river, this time for the Mississippi River Commission as the boss of a gang of ex-Mississippi and Louisiana convicts and as a member of a survey party on the Mississippi River. As before, the whirling waters and romance of the river made for a meaningful experience for Clark.

Many years later he would remember those days with great warmth. "The old rivermen aboard had a glimmer of the spots passed, and it was with deep nostalgia that they watched it disappear. These hard-bitten rivermen knew a lot about the river and the lore of steamboats. For me it was an exciting experience to hear their stories told, not so much in a historical context, but rather as an intimate part of the webs of their own lives. They spoke of the old, not once but many times. There was no greater thrill than to view these places from the perspective of a steamboat pilothouse and to hear about them from a pilot who had to know them by heart or run his boat aground. At night the drowsy Texas decks became folk forums in which men dredged up the past. To me the endless procession of oil and grain barges that plowed their way downstream brought with them the air of romance which cloaked their muddy and oily decks. I knew about Mark Twain, Huckleberry Finn, and Tom Sawyer--I had read the books. It was another thing, however, to be awakened at night by a lonely leadsman at the head of a tow calling out the twain marks."

The land, the rivers, and the man--all coming together with the books and the quad to form the complete historian.

At the close of his undergraduate work at Ole Miss, Clark applied for and received a scholarship in the graduate school of the University of Kentucky.

He also had the option of attending the University of Cincinnati.

So he flipped a coin.

By such a fateful toss the state of Ohio lost an invaluable human resource.

When Thomas Clark completed his master thesis in Lexington on the subject of trade between Kentucky and the lower South, he decided to do his doctoral work in yet another southern state--North Carolina.

Just as the oppressive cloud of the Great Depression was first settling upon this nation, the aspiring young historian headed for newly established Duke University. There he received his Ph.D. in 1932 after completing his dissertation on "The Development of Railways in the Southwestern and Adjacent States Before 1860". This was a subject he tackled with great enthusiasm, but which wore down to a tedious and unexcited finish.

Thus the academic training of this formidable scholar criss-crossed his beloved southland, lending a deeper sense of people and places to his learning.

In the midst of this country's most trying economic times, Clark left Duke in 1931 and obtained a teaching job back at the University of Kentucky. Two years later he married pretty Martha Elizabeth Turner whom he had met while at Durham. Elizabeth, a South Carolinian with well educated and progressive parents, had been working as a librarian at Duke University when she met the young graduate student.

Once settled back in the Bluegrass as a family man, Clark pursued his original interest and in 1937 published his *History Of Kentucky*--a work which would become the classic textbook of Kentucky's schools.

He was a prolific writer. Soon to follow were *The Rampaging Frontier, The Kentucky*--which was a part of the Rivers of America series--*Pills, Petticoats, and Plows,* and *The Southern Country Editor.*

A list of the major works of Thomas D. Clark is shown at the close of this book.

Outstanding and productive as he was as a writer, his first loves were his family and teaching, in that order.

His and Elizabeth's eldest child, Thomas Bennett Clark, was born in Lexington in 1936. Their daughter, Ruth Elizabeth, followed three years later. Both of the children received much intellectual stimulation and attention from their parents, and shared the many trips throughout the United States and overseas.

In the university community the transplanted Mississippian flourished. Another Kentucky historian, Holman Hamilton, later wrote: "Instructor Clark, who in 1935 became Assistant Professor Clark, one in whom (President) McVey found hope and promise. A splendid lecturer, human and humorous, he became one of the campus' most popular teachers. It was not, however, a cheap popularity. Virile, handsome, searching, quizzical, he could be incisive, far-ranging, eloquent, earthy--arousing genuine interest on the part of his students, many of whom never forgot him."

So Professor Clark settled in at the University of Kentucky to make his mark. In 1942, the thirty-eight year old Clark was selected as the head of the department of history. From then until 1965, he charged forward to literally transform what had been a lethargic and undistinguished department into one of national reputation and one of the strongest in the south. He brought in new teachers with wide ranging experience and expertise expanding the curriculum with numerous specialized historical subjects.

And he encouraged his colleagues to write--and to publish. Instructing and writing were both necessary, in his opinion, to round out the complete teacher.

Clark was rounded out even further by his international assignments.

In 1950 he went to Europe where he taught for half a year as professor at the University of Vienna. Two years earlier he had been invited to Salzburg, Austria to be a staff member of the internationally famous Salzburg Seminar. In 1952 he received an unusually interesting assignment from the U. S. State Department for conducting a series of lectures over several months time in India. He lectured in other overseas assignments before spending a semester in Greece in the late 60's as a professor at the Universities of Athens and Thessalonica.

And on and on it goes, this myriad of human experiences--both academic and practical.

Thomas Clark has never retired. Even today, he serves on numerous boards and is active in both his own individual research as well as speaking to and assisting various historical societies and clubs.

And of course he continues to write.

He and Elizabeth still live in the large two story house, which they built in 1939, on a picturesque tree-lined street in Lexington. The years have not diminished their warm and gracious manner of living, and now they are story book grandparents.

What impresses one the most today about this engaging sage is his intellectual vim and vigor. As one will see in these pages, he is a man of history but not shackled to the past. His life may span the greater part of this century, but his spirit and intellect is young and futuristic.

Thomas Clark is an old man--and he's proud of that word "old"--with the mind, heart, and zest of a college junior.

And that is one reason he is such a valuable resource. He is not just fit for the spinning of tales of yore. But he can address the issues of today with conviction and insight.

The purpose of this book is to provide a "feel" for the man, his time and place.

To be a Southerner, we learn from Clark, can still be a marked distinction. There are no stars and bars in his study; no artifacts of the rebel gray. But his life distills the essence of the South--its gracious manner, fierce pride, and a new enlightenment. Clark reminds us--and reminds all narrow minded people on both sides of the Mason Dixon line--that the Confederate cause was only a part of the South as a diseased tooth is of the whole body. It is painful and creates lasting memories of woe, but once extracted, the body moves on with all its healthy parts.

In short, Clark is the quintessence of enlightenment, proclaiming in his teaching and writings that the southern man and woman--the Kentucky man and woman--can preserve and maintain southern civility and charm without being obsessed with the rancor of the past.

But then again, Thomas Clark may be an endangered species, a vanishing American.

For as he states in this book, America is becoming more and more a homogenous whole. One can travel the entire breadth of this country and speak the same language, eat at the same chain restaurants, sleep in identical motels, and buy gas from the same company. From Boston to Santa Fe, people are growing more and more alike in their interests and values. "In a country of highly varied climate and terrain," Phillip Langdon has written in the *Atlantic* magazine, "thousands of cities and towns now look as if they were put together with interchangeable parts." Thus with the breaking down of the sectional walls of this country, the regional man--his distinct personality deeply attuned to the land and the people--may eventually disappear from the national landscape. In reality there may be no more easterner, mid-westerner--or southerner.

But this prospect must come back around to encounter another trend in the country which seems to be leading us back to our roots, to our own ethnic and cultural uniqueness. The more we become the same, it seems, the more we strive to be different, to stand apart, to have our own corner of the world where we are proud of our peculiar identity.

Thomas Clark, the southerner--the Kentuckian--helps us find our way. He understands where we have been, where we are, and where we are probably going.

This book, filled with his thoughts, his reflections, his writings, and his conversation, represents only a modicum of the man.

And the man represents a great part of us all.

Henry David Thoreau was thinking of men like Clark

when he wrote, "The frontiers are not east or west, north or south; but wherever man fronts a fact."

The secret to Thomas Clark's perpetual wit, sparkle and charm is that he resides on that lingering frontier.

TRACES OF THE OLD ORDER

"The modern South stands astride the great divide. Behind it lie both the nineteenth century and the first half of the twentieth, eras marked by crisis and frustration. Essentially southern history has been marred by conflict: conflict between the sections; between a predominantly agricultural society competing in a rising industrial age; between political approaches and points of view; between two races sharing a common regional heritage and competing for economic survival on a common ground; and, finally, conflicts engendered by defeat in a Civil War and the impasse of a chaotic period of reconstruction. A region thus caught in the travail of time has created many images by which it has expressed both hopes and sentiments. Some of these have been the deeply sentimental ones of the so-called "moonlight and roses" concept of better days in the past. Others have symbolized bitter racial friction, economic frustrations, and lost leadership and waste of human resources.

Whatever images the region has accepted, they have been familiar social landmarks in the past. One image which ranks high but undefined is the constant reverence for the southern heritage or southern way of life. Like every broad generalization this one makes a deep emotional appeal but gives a poorly defined sense of direction. Far too many southerners have accepted these generalities as images of regional peace and well-being without realizing that the South, like every other area of the world, lives in an era of deep-seated and fundamental change. Almost without realizing what they do, great masses of southern people have accepted forces which revolutionize their lives without understanding that they also destroy old images."

B. C.: *It may come as a surprise to many to learn that you are not a native Kentuckian, but a product of Mississippi. Tell us about your family.*

T. C.: My parents were John Collingsworth Clark and Sallie Bennett Clark--members of two old pioneer families. The Bennetts came from Charleston, South Carolina, emigrated by way of the Atlantic Coast around to--well, my great grandfather came from Mobile up the Tombigbee River, and then across to Winston County, Mississippi. My Clark relatives were Virginians who came from the neighborhood of the lower James River Valley.

They followed the typical southern emigration path up to Prince Edward County, and from there they turned south. Instead of coming on here to Kentucky as thousands of families did, they went south to Anderson County, South Carolina. In 1834, four Clark brothers set out for the cotton lands of Mississippi, land which had just been freed by the Dancing Rabbit Treaty.

It took them about five or six years, as nearly as I can determine, to go from Anderson, South Carolina, to Louisville, Mississippi. It is no trick at all now to drive it in eight hours, and it took them all those years to go across. They grew crops as they went along. They settled down at the head of the Pearl River, and there, my great-grandfather John Collingsworth Clark, who was born in South Carolina, built a large, double log house.

All that country down there was settled largely by South Carolinians with a generous sprinkling of North Carolinians. They brought along to the lower south the old Carolina-style "dog-trot" house. I was born in the same room in which my grandfather was born. This pioneer house stood until I went to college, then it caught on fire and burned. It was a landmark house in the community.

I was born and raised on a cotton farm. All of my family were farmers. I had two sisters and three brothers. We've always been land owners. They could have acquired land--thousands of acres of it--for a minimal expenditure. Yet my people remained yeoman farmers. There wasn't a whole lot of social and economic difference in the situation of people in our county. We didn't have any rich people, we didn't have any big slave-holders or large plantation owners. We had none of the stuff that is considered the romantic way of life in the old South. Thank God we didn't. We came up in a community of people such as those described by Frank L. Owsley in his book, *Plain People of the Old South*, or those described in A. B. Longstreet's *Georgia Scenes*. They were Protestants. They were Anglo-American--I don't really like to use the word "Anglo-Saxon"--but they were homogenous as to ethnic background. Three religious denominations prevailed--Baptists, Methodists, and Presbyterians. My people felt that they had to have the damp hand of Wesleyanism on their infantile heads--they were strong Methodists. My father's mother was a staunch Baptist and, as a matter of fact, her father gave the land on which the main Baptist Church stands in the present town of Louisville, Mississippi. But these people all spoke with a common accent, a common idiom and vernacular, and from a common experience background. They brought with them in their emigration parties an enormous amount of folklore, folk ways, and an inexhaustible ability to adapt to a harsh, crude way of life. They did do so, happily I think. I think if I had to go back and experience some of the things they did, I might find the going exceedingly rough, but they adapted to it and they were reasonably happy.

B. C.: What is the most vivid memory that you have of growing up in Mississippi in the early part of the century?

T. C.: First, I grew up in a close-knit family in which blood ran thick. Family connections--that great, sprawling concentric circle of kinship--cousins down to God knows where--to tenth cousins, we were all kin. That family has proven a lasting sentimental memory. That was a very deep, intimate, personal thing.

The second thing that impressed me deeply--personally, although not so much professionally--was the Civil War. If I had actually gone through the battles of the war, they couldn't have been any more vivid to me than they were. We had members of the family who were old Confederate soldiers. All you had to do was go out the front door and throw a rock and you would either hit an ex-slave or a Confederate veteran. Our neighbors were Confederate veterans, and I went to the Confederate reunions. We read Confederate books. The "cause" to us was not only a right political one--we couldn't distinguish between the "cause" of the Christian religion and the "cause" of the Confederacy. They were both sacred causes with an equal degree of personal and emotional meaning.

B. C.: Were they intertwined?

T. C.: Yes. I say that with some hesitation. Yes, I suppose they were. They were intertwined in the sense that they were moral causes. We considered it--without all the political, theoretical innuendos, all of the historical considerations--we simply considered it from the viewpoint of the veterans. They thought they were fighting a "Holy War". I've often wondered what two of my uncles--great-uncles--had in their minds when they joined the Confederate army. What triggered their actions? They joined a volunteer Mississippi regiment and marched straight off to war without any preparation, and with very poor equipment. They virtually enlisted and went immediately into the battle of Shiloh. One of them was shot in the stomach, ran around the church and fell on the steps of the church and died. The other one lived through the war and went away to Texas. Only within the last ten years has the family rediscovered its Texas branch.

A third thing that made a lasting impression, not only on my mind but on my spiritual being, if you can differentiate between the two, was the wilderness country. My county was heavily wooded, deeply forested, still virgin land and virgin timber. Somewhere in my emotional make-up I found myself attuned to the raw nature about me. Just think of that wonderful--I can hardly believe it today--that wonderful virgin forest with its magnificent pines--those great pine trees that had stood there for centuries. I am not sure how long. A lot longer time than I shall ever live. But certainly they had lived a century or more. I saw those wonderful woods as a child and they stood just like ancient monuments of time really. I can take you right now within twenty feet of where some of the noblest trees stood. There were the pine woods with their neighboring impenetrable stand of hard wood, and then there were the swamps. We lived at the headwaters of the Pearl River and we could live in both the hill country or the swamps. They were intertwined.

Imagine those big canebrakes. It has been many days since I have seen canebrakes such as those that I saw in my childhood. Then there were all the animals that went with virgin forests: deer, turkeys, wild hogs, and the small game, plus fur-bearing animals.

B. C.: What exactly is a "canebrake"?

T. C.: I'm glad you asked about that. I will try to differentiate between the Kentucky canebrake and true Mississippi ones. Much of the cane in Kentucky was relatively small. It was trim cane, all right, and it grew taller than a man, but it never got to be very large-bodied. It never got up much beyond the fishing pole stage. You had, as nearly as I can tell from reading the pioneer records, very thick cane. In places it created a very heavy ground cover which was dangerous on the one hand, because it was ideal hiding grounds for Indians. On the other, it was a positive advantage because it attracted heavy herbivorous animals to this region. I see cane along creeks here in Kentucky, and I can show you a lot of cane growing along the banks of streams that never gets larger than three-quarters of an inch in diameter. That is, I've never seen it up over that size.

I think if this country were completely deserted and allowed to go back to nature, much of it would once more become covered in cane. The canebrakes I knew as a boy in Mississippi were entirely different. Whether they were botanically different, I don't know. But that was large cane. It got up to an inch and a half and some of it got up to two inches in diameter. It grew very thick. To get lost in a big canebrake was a frightening experience, and was hazardous. I have read stories of people becoming badly confused, and it was dangerous for several reasons. If you fell down in there and fell on one of the sharp stubble or ends, they'd cut you like a knife. Canebrakes were havens for rattlesnakes. Rattlesnakes liked the cover. Within one-hundred yards from where I was born was a tremendous canebrake. It, of course, was associated with the Choctaw Indians. I came up in country where Choctaw Indians were almost as commonplace as white settlers. As you know, when the United States Government removed the Indians from that country after the signing of the Dancing Rabbit Treaty (1830), many of them took to the swamps and remained behind. They are still there. It is not an unusual sight to see an Indian in central Mississippi, around Philadelphia, and Dekalb, or in Louisville.

B. C.: How did the Confederate veterans consider the rebellion and the War Between the States a "Holy War" whenever the cause they espoused included the enslavement of an entire race of people?

T. C.: There is a paradox, a very decided paradox. I'll use my family as an example. You could pick at random any of those country families and you'd have the same thing.

When my family migrated from Virginia down into the Carolinas, across Georgia and Alabama, and into Central Mississippi, they did two things that fascinate me tremendously. One, they followed a thermal corridor. The rainfall varied very little between Anderson, South Carolina, and Louisville, Mississippi. Around 52 inches annual rainfall in both places, and the temperature was practically the same. It was a little hotter, but very little so, during the extreme heat months of July and August, and early September, in Central Mississippi than in Anderson,

South Carolina. How did they know about that thermal route? What kept them in the trough or in that corridor? All these people knew about the weather was what they could observe in the clouds or read in the ancient folk signs. They were pretty good predictors of the weather at that. Their knowledge of weather lore came from a very long and varied experience, folk experience, in dealing with the weather and nature. The second thing, in moving through that Carolina-Georgia-Alabama corridor, they almost moved completely clear of the slave belt. The corridor they went through had the lightest slave population almost of any part of the eastern slave belt, that is, the area east of the Mississippi River. My people had, as nearly as I can tell, only one or two slaves. At most, they might have had five or six. When they did have slaves, it was hard to distinguish between the slave family and the white family, because they lived pretty much on the same plane. It was a family affair. We had no plantations. I could not name you a single plantation in my home county that was comparable to the romantic concept of the southern slave-cotton plantation. There were people who owned maybe a thousand acres of land, but their way of life was not any different, really, from their smaller land-holder neighbors. So slavery in my home community was never considered--prior to the Civil War--a nefarious and evil institution.

The slave population was in the minority of the white population after the war, of course. There were ex-slaves, and I knew some of them. There was a woman named Aunt Betsy Harper, who had once belonged to the Harper family in Frankfort, Kentucky. She had been sold into the slave trade out of Kentucky. She lived on our place, and then her children and grandchildren either lived there or in the neighborhood. Aunt Betsy ruled her roost. She was a white-haired, dignified woman with a high temper. I remember one time she was whipping one of her grandchildren unmercifully and my father made her stop, and she delivered him a long lecture on how no account her grandchildren were.

We had other ex-slaves in our community. Two of them were Uncle Silas and Jeremiah Miller. These men were

Congo slaves, born in Africa. The Miller ex-slaves had belonged to a family of the same name, and the interesting thing about them was they remained intensely loyal to the members of that white family. They chopped and picked cotton for us. A lot of times we took a wagon and a pair of mules and would go up to the Miller settlement and pick up as many hands as could crowd into the wagon and bring them down to chop cotton and in the fall they came back to pick cotton. There were not any ex-slaves among them, but they were the children and grandchildren of ex-slaves. On occasions, I would go to get them and they were unable to work for us because their former Miller masters needed something done and they would drop anything and everything they were doing to help those people. They remained intensely loyal to their former white families. As far as I know, the Miller descendants remained intensely loyal to them. Theirs was a close-knit amicable relationship.

Now, there was another ex-slave named Uncle Sam Metts, who was a character. He belonged to a Confederate officer named Captain Michael Metts. Uncle Sam went to the Civil War as a body servant to Captain Metts. When the war was over, the Captain came home about as poor as Uncle Sam. He could not maintain his former slaves legally, of course, and he could not have financially at that point anyway. Uncle Sam, some way or another, drifted onto my Grandfather Bennett's farm. We had Metts around us until--well, it hasn't been long even now since some member of my family has not had one of those Metts on their farm doing something for them. They come to see my sisters occasionally. When I go home, she will point out a black man to me and say, "That's one of the Metts."

Well, Uncle Sam was a character. He cooked for my mother. During those hard years of 1905 and 1906, my father moved to a sawmill village and my mother kept a boarding house. My father drove a logging team. He was the most unlikely human being on all the face of the globe to be a logger. I cannot imagine my father being in the log woods with an ox team, but he was. When my mother moved away from the mill, they had no further need for Uncle Sam's services.

That was not the end of Uncle Sam. He paid us frequent visits, always coming to ask if we didn't have a ham bone or something. He knew he would go home with something because we just inherited him. He was ours. We had to take care of him, and at times the whole tribe, until I left the farm. There were Metts there and there were other ex-slave descendants.

B. C.: Did you ever talk to any ex-slaves that had come across on slave ships?

T. C.: Uncle Sam and Uncle Silas and his brother, Jeremiah--they came over on a slave ship in perhaps as late as 1850.

B. C.: Did they ever relate any of their experiences?

T. C.: I did not know enough to ask them. I have wished many times that I might have had the intelligence to ask them about their experiences.

B. C.: So, the perception of the war being a "Holy War" as far as the advancement and preservation of slavery was concerned, was considered by these Confederate veterans to be a gallant defense of the family unit, including the slave member?

T. C.: And also homeland. They were heavily propagandized, as you can imagine. When the cotton barons met in those famous conventions and discussed the problems, and later on when the whole secession issue was argued, the common people of the South were almost oblivious to all that. They almost knew nothing, theoretically, about the secession and its legalistic issues.

B. C.: You're talking about the majority of the people?

T. C.: Yes, that side of the intensive slave-holding belt. What they did know, and were highly sensitized about, was the possibility of the invasion of their homeland and they themselves being oppressed. They were yeoman farmers, nevertheless.

I feel certain that the people in my section of Mississippi were heavily influenced in the reactions of the old South Carolina social and political attitudes. Their folk culture and attitudes reflected their immediate past emigrant history. They were a highly independent people. There has never been a frontiersman in North America more ruggedly independent. Sometimes they were illiterate and ignorant, and of course provincial. They were isolated geographically and politically as far as ready communication with the broader world about them was concerned. But these were decent common people well attuned to their way of life. They knew little if anything about any other way of life. They were not going to have their lives disrupted if they could help it. This is a basic conclusion which I think can be sustained. Else, why did the non-slaveholders rush off to war so willingly and so quickly without knowing where they were going, and without having any realistic concept whatsoever of their approaching fate? I think you could say that about nearly every social and economic level of southerners, or as for that matter, for the whole nation.

I do not think that the people of my community were fiercely defensive of slavery. They could not have had a very heavy financial or economic stake in it. Those who owned slaves in my home county had only small numbers, sometimes no more than a family or two.

B. C.: Do you think that was the general sentiment among a majority of the Southerners?

T. C.: I do not know the answer to that one. Take Mississippi for instance. Mississippi is a highly sectionalized state. Just east of our home was the Alabama Black Belt. My home county is just one county in from Alabama and removed by swamplands from the edge of the Black Belt and the Tombigbee River Valley. The prairie belt in Mississippi spreads over the area of Columbus, Macon, and extends as far north as Tupelo. Popularly it is called prairie country. Geologically, it is the so-called Alabama Black Belt because of the composition of the soil and the type of plantation farming. That was the major slave belt nearest my home county. Columbus still has the remains of the old slave-holding antebellum South with the big houses and a certain appearance of affluence. Well, to the southwest of us was the Natchez, Vicksburg, and Mississippi Valley areas with their intensive slave populations. And immediately west of us was the Mississippi Delta. This Mississippi Delta is in the Yazoo Valley and a distinctly marked area sociologically, geologically, geographically, and economically. That was a rapidly rising slave belt. The population was becoming overwhelmingly black slaves. In between were the southern Piney Woods, a region which had almost no slaves. That was the southern hills or the coastal plain that extended into the central hill country where I was born and raised. It was lightly populated by slaves. There was another small section called the Flat Woods with fairly sterile land that had a sparse population. Again, Mississippi is a highly sectionalized state.

B. C.: Since a majority of the people did not own slaves, wasn't secession over the slave issue more of a movement of the upper class than it was for the middle and lower class?

T. C.: Surely. My people had very little stake in slavery as an economic institution.

B. C.: In your opinion, had the secession question been put to a popular vote in your community and throughout the South, would the Confederate states have seceded from the Union?

T. C.: I do not believe that they would have, had the subject been presented to them logically and without emotion. I have often wondered about their reactions. If somebody had come to my home county and said, "Now, here are the alternatives, here are the options", I think, unless some hothead got in and stirred them up, that they would have calmly said, "We will go with the established order." These people were just establishing themselves. My home section was still frontier country. The people who had only recently arrived there were just establishing themselves economically and in every other area that organized communities were being formed.

I want to go back to something more about the differences between a yeoman farm and a plantation. I am a cold realist and I think I've had experience enough that I can say that. I have visited many old plantations in the heavy slave belts around Natchez, Vicksburg, and Charleston, and Columbia, South Carolina and Savannah, Georgia. I remember once visiting the Middleton Plantation in South Carolina. While my wife was touring the grounds and buildings, I speculated if I could have come to this plantation this morning as manager or owner and had to face all the realities that confronted the former owners, would I take that option? My answer would be, "No, never. No." They were caught up to a large extent in a situation that they could not escape. Realistically, they were so deeply involved financially and emotionally that they could not very well get out. They were enslaved by the system itself. I am sure that many a plantation owner got up many mornings wondering how he was going to solve some of the problems that confronted him.

Now, I grew up in cotton country. All my people were cotton farmers, but none were big cotton producers. I not only grew up in the yeoman cotton farm system, but I also have managed a plantation of my own. Once I got into the pine land business, I had nothing to do with cotton. I took over the management of an old cotton plantation and planted it in pines. Even then I could not escape the nagging management problems. There were no slaves and overseers to worry about. There was just one thing after another in the management of a plantation that ordinary human beings don't think about. When you see all these romantic projections of women in hoop skirts and men in frock-tailed coats congregated in elegant drawing rooms and riding on steamboats and having a big time, that was only a part of the story. No doubt some did. No doubt the upper level of antebellum society did a generous amount of socializing. But when it came down to the nitty-gritty of operating a cotton plantation day in and day out with slave labor, you are talking about something very real and demanding indeed.

I have just reread W. J. Cash's *Mind of the South.* I don't agree with him in many things he says, but I'm tremendously interested in his attempt to define the social class "Southern aristocracy". That was a pretty superficial group after all, based upon a pretty shaky foundation in the main. It was a snobbish thing to begin with. I personally do not come from that background.

B. C.: That hasn't changed much. There's still a certain amount of that even here in Kentucky.

T. C.: Surely, surely. You take this Bluegrass farming tradition and especially the horse farms which harbor the rich and the near rich. Historically, the so-called bluegrass aristocracy has been a minor fact inside of the state's economy. On that rich farm land in Western Kentucky there arose a class of prosperous land owners. They have often been spokesmen in political affairs and have wielded power all out of proportion to their just desserts and numbers. Surely, that's happened time in and time out.

B. C.: What, in your opinion, would have happened to the institution of slavery had there not been the Civil War?

T. C.: You're asking a complex question which has been asked countless times. Historians have speculated about this matter over and over again. First, let me qualify anything I might say that might make me appear utterly foolish. I try to be a historian, at least, and I don't like to get into the "ifs" of human natures, because the moment a historian begins "ifing" he's departed from the possibility of documenting what he's saying--he doesn't know any more than anybody else. After I have said that, I guess most historians who have thought seriously on this subject have concluded mainly three or four things.

First, the rising technological age in America--the rising mechanical age--coming out of the 1830's and 1840's and

1850's inevitably would have created intense competition which the slave system couldn't have withstood. The rise of the east-west transportation system, railways, telegraph lines and the improvement of the eastern canal system and rivers was rapidly isolating the South economically. The South was well nigh helpless to offer much competition in this rising competitive commercial-mechanical-technological age. Cheap labor came to this country with the enormous immigration from Europe during the 1870's and 1880's. Of course, had there not been a Civil War, immigration might well have been heavier during the 1860's than it was. With expansion of this country and more free western states being admitted, the South politically would have lost leadership ground in the Congress and in the electoral or administrative and executive offices. The South had enjoyed a political predominence in national political affairs, but by 1850 it was definitely becoming a minority. That is the handwriting I think you can read, in retrospect, being written on the wall. Slavery was becoming inefficient and just downright trifling and wasteful as a system of labor.

The second point I want to make is, not all Southerners, by any manner of means, looked upon slavery as a beneficial human institution. There was a large segment of society that had nothing to do with slavery. These people would have gotten rid of it. They looked upon it as a sapping, devitalizing social force inside a free society.

Thirdly, I think there would have been less dependence upon a stable crop, such as sugar or tobacco or rice, certainly cotton. Each year, more and more competition was rising in the field of cotton production abroad. India, Egypt, and other cotton producing areas of the world were having an impact on Southern cotton productions.

Finally, I think the financial system, the matter of credit, of financing an enormously expensive plantation system with all the uncertainties that went along with producing a crop--that system would have broken down.

These are some of the areas that historians have dwelt on. I think that if the sociology and the economics of the situation had been allowed a free contemporary play, slavery as an institution would have simply disappeared. It might not have disappeared completely or all at once. There no doubt would have been a lingering vestige of household slavery, would not have mattered to much.

B. C.: How long do you think that phase would have lingered?

T. C.: Oh, a couple of decades or so, maybe half a century.

B. C.: Do you think that by the turn of the century, either by state or Federal legislative action or at the behest of slave owners themselves, slavery would have vanished from the American scene?

T. C.: How would you like to have had a family on your hands, where you had to be responsible for their sustenance and health, for clothing and housing them, and for their general welfare? How would you like to face that? You would have been hard pressed. I think it was unfortunate that in the 1830's the slavery issue took a turn in a different direction from what it had pursued earlier. The anti-slavery movement was cast on a moral ground. Abolitionists made moral issues of it, making Southerners appear to be immoral people for maintaining the institution of slavery. Right down to the outbreak of the Civil War itself and on through Reconstruction, that particular aspect of racial attitudes and racial relations had strong moral accusative overtones. Now, I am not a slave historian. I make no pretense whatsoever of being a historian of slavery. Such writings by the authors of *Time On The Cross*, and numerous essays, books and documentary collections have been produced since the 1960's on slavery. In fact, the literature on slavery has become most voluminous, and you can find all these straws blowing in that wind regarding the things that I have talked about.

But what I'm saying is that the economic and financial argument against slavery, not the social or political one, would have eventually been the snags bringing its demise.

Standing in a class talking about this period in American history, the simplest thing you could have said was that the moral issue of slavery caused the Civil War. The hardest position you could have ever taken was to defend that proposition. The causes of the Civil War were very complex and many. They were rooted in all sorts of issues--economic and commercial. And there was the lack of understanding among the sections.

More directly related to the war were the issues of the Missouri Compromise, the Kansas-Nebraska Debate, and the Dred Scott Decision. You can even go back and pick up the frightening slave insurrections such as the Denmark Vesey uprising or the Nat Turner rebellion. There was that aspect of fear. I knew very directly the fear of race riots. I grew up in a community where there was constant talk about the possibility of such a disturbance. That fear was very real. I can appreciate what a tremor of excitement the Denmark Vesey or the Nat Turner rebellion touched off.

B. C.: Then it all revolved around and comes back to the issue of slavery, don't you think?

T. C.: It's hard to steer away from that. Slavery was at the basis of so many southern and national issues and the making of so many decisions, and so deeply impacted on the Southern system. It is so hard to get around that.

B. C.: What if the South had successfully seceded and had won the War? What would have been the future of this fragmented country?

T. C.: Heavens, I don't know the answer to that. I can only nibble around the edges of this question. Primarily, we would have created one hellofa state of confusion in trade. There would have been trade barriers and trade confusions with all the regulatory confusions between the sections of the continent.

Well, there wouldn't have been a nation. I think we would have had political chaos within the South itself over the wielding of power. I think there would have been grim dissatisfaction with a lot of things that happened in the South. It is hard for me to conceive of the South operating as an independent nation. I simply do not know what would have happened. It's hard for me to conceive of that.

B. C.: Were the cultural and social ties between North and South that were severed during the Civil War nevertheless strong enough that the South would have voluntarily rejoined the Nation at a later date? Out of national security, perhaps?

T. C.: They might have been. There's a thing which has always impressed me about the situation that might have arisen with an independent southern nation. The South would have been dependent upon Britain for a market for its cotton. It would have been dependent also upon the North for a market for its cotton and other goods, and as a source of supply of manufactured materials. The big thing was that the South was undercapitalized as far as banking and credit facilities were available in the region. It was solely dependent on outside capital sources. If it had set up as an independent nation, it would have been faced with one terrific tax burden to maintain it. It would have been faced with a severe need for capital structure and capital operations. Could it have established an industrial system? Could it have supported an urban spread of cities? Could it have created cities that could have been commercially sustained as an independent nation? It certainly would have caused a lot of refocusing on numerous priorities for the South. There's no doubt about that. I wish I knew the answer to this question. It is intriguing, but it did not happen. There are a lot of times in these things in history that you almost wish things might have happened differently so that you might know the answer to those kinds of questions.

B. C.: Was the Civil War inevitable?

T. C.: I think after 1850 it became increasingly inevitable.

B. C.: Could things have been done prior to 1850 to avoid it?

T. C.: I don't know the answer to that one. I would have to take out proper insurance here. It would have helped if the abolitionists had softened their crusade and they had been less accusative.

The second thing would have been--I think this would have been tremendously important but maybe impossible--to have concentrated upon developing the transportation system between the North and the South and a direct commercial integration between the two sections. This is just a statement of hopeless idealism. If lesser ambitious and self-willed men had sat down calmly and looked at this thing and said, "We are heading for chaos unless we take certain precautionary measures," it might have been different. In westward expansion, for instance, if there had been a little leeway for the expansion of slavery, war might have been avoided. The American people would have saved all that commotion, all the emotions that were aroused by the Compromise of 1850, the Kansas-Nebraska Act, the Lincoln-Douglas Debates, the Dred Scott Decision, and then the acts of the secessionists and hotheads. There again we are dealing with "ifs". It did not happen that way. We had the poison in our system and we had to get it out. There was one hellofa lot of bloodshed, plus a lot of lost time, loss of national momentum, loss of morale, loss of so many things of human value.

B. C.: Do you believe that there still exists today a misunderstanding between the North and South?

T. C.: Yes, there is no doubt about that. I'm not much disturbed about that personally. The most provincial place that I know anything about is New York City. I guess you could say it is also the most cosmopolitan place you could find. You go to New England and there is a distinct mind set there. You go into the Middle West and there again you have a situation that's sometimes hard to define. Out on the west coast is another situation. However, we have also drawn closer together. We have developed such an intricate and efficient system of transportation--highways that penetrate all parts of the nation--that we're not living in isolated regions anymore. It would be hard to isolate a section of the nation--nearly impossible. We have become so interdependent on the intersectional system that we could ill afford to disrupt it in our present daily affairs of life.

We have become such a standardized people. We may react sectionally to certain issues, but you go into a town in New England and suddenly you get on a plane and go to a town in Texas and what do you see? The same chain stores, same shopping malls, the same standardized brands, the same banking hours, the same type of public school systems, and you can go right down the list. Aside from a few local peculiarities, we are a highly standardized and homogenized people. That breaks down our regional distinctness. Take our banking system. The national banking system--the Federal Reserve--has such tight control over the fiscal affairs of the nation that you could almost bankrupt any section that undertook to do any hanky-panky by just simply allowing the Federal Reserve system to go after it in a hurry. Not only that, but the commercial banking system is as intimately tied up with the affairs of New Orleans as in Boston. It is a throttle hold on fiscal affairs not only of this nation but of the world. Our communication system is instantaneous. They do not know anything in New York City that we do not know in Drip Rock, Kentucky--that is if the television newscasts have any validity. We no longer have pockets of isolation or provincialism.

Of course, the South has certain peculiar assets. In the South we enjoy climate which is reasonably good. I wouldn't be so foolish as to say that we have a perfect climate, we do not. We have extremely hot and we can have some extremely cold weather. But generally speaking, we have a pretty even climate. And in the last few years the Sun Belt has been a growing factor. People come south to enjoy the climate. The South has resources that are renewable. It has a lot of resources that can be exhausted. It has an enormous forestry resource that is readily renewable.

The region has an abundance of water. We have abused it; we have abused it terribly. We can renew our water system. We have soil which has been terribly abused. But one thing about it also--much of the Southern soil can be reclaimed and renewed. We have some other distinct advantages. We have cheap transportation in our water systems. The Mississippi River, the Tennessee Valley, the Tombigbee system, the Cumberland and Tennessee rivers, and the eastern intercoastal canal system give us great water transportation. And we are developing a very good highway system. I would say that it is a superb highway system. So, I've seen the South in my time come completely out of an isolated, land-locked, mud-locked, one crop system, into one which is steadily becoming a rapidly industrialized, urbanized and capitalized region.

B. C.: Tell me about your interest in history and how you developed it.

T. C.: First of all, I was born on the raw frontier. As I told you earlier, it was a wonder that I did not become a Civil War historian, with all the talk of the war and all the old veterans living nearby and reminiscing about the war. And the fact that they felt so passionately and my people felt so passionately about the war, it is a wonder that I did not become a Civil War historian. Strangely, I never had any great fascination with battles. In fact, I have a very poor concept of battles. I have never latched onto a Civil War hero as a biographical subject. My interest has been more in the land and the people.

My mother had gone to college and she had a very real interest in reading. We got together, surprisingly, a fairly good miscellaneous assortment of books. That was amazing in that cotton country. My Grandfather Bennett also had a right good collection of books. I read those with much interest. I started reading at an early age--I read everything I could lay my hands on. And then, I was raised in a community where things happened, like the Dancing Rabbit Treaty. Also there was the visit of Tecumseh--Tecumseh came to within twenty miles of my home on his famous visit south. He might have actually come by my home because he visited the Choctaw village of Mashualaville. We lived just off the Jackson Military Road, or the Robinson branch of this famous road. We were not far from the Natchez Trace, and although that seemed like pretty sterile country to the outsiders, there were a lot of things that happened there. I was fascinated with the Choctaw Indians and knew nothing about how they had been discriminated against.

B. C.: So you acquired this love for history at a very early age?

T. C.: I did. I did reading and had historic places and things all around me. When I went to the university I became acquainted with Charles S. Sydnor, who turned out to be one of the really important historians of the South. I never really had any significant courses under Professor Sydnor. I had one brief course in British History, but none on the South or American History. He and I remained very close friends throughout his lifetime. He was at Ole Miss--the University of Mississippi--and later when I went to Duke University, Sydnor was very interested in that school. They were paying him a starvation salary at Ole Miss when he was appointed a professor at Duke. I do not know how he got there or anything about that.

B. C.: You graduated from the University of Mississippi with a degree in history, and then you worked on your Masters at Duke?

T. C.: I went to Duke in the fall of 1929. But Charlie Sydnor--in conversations in the halls at Ole Miss--encouraged me to study history. Many times I would stop to talk with this young professor. The more I talked with him the more I became interested in being a historian.

I became certain that I did not want to become a lawyer. It was not that I did not like the law and did not want to be a lawyer, it simply was the fact that I guess I had more interest in history.

B. C.: This was toward the end of your undergraduate study?

T. C.: Yes. In fact, it was throughout my whole undergraduate years.

B. C.: So, you changed from being a lawyer to wanting to be a historian and a teacher?

T. C.: That's right. All that--too, Sydnor encourged me to go to graduate school. I did not know much about graduate school or advanced study, to tell you the truth. I knew practically nothing about it. But he said if I wanted to be a historian I should become trained. I applied, as I told you, for this scholarship here at the University of Kentucky. To these people here at Kentucky, I owe a great deal--but here I had one or two of the worst professors that I could imagine. But I have to be honest and say that they did stimulate my interest in going on.

In the spring of 1929, I made application for scholarships--I made a lot of applications--and got little ones here and there. At Wisconsin for instance, I got a tuition scholarship. I got one at Missouri and I got a very good one at Vanderbilt. But I was frightened by that one because Dean Walter Lynnwood Fleming was in a faltering mental state at that time. He would write me letters that would sound erratic--they were almost meaningless letters. Then the Duke scholarship came along and I accepted it.

B. C.: And that was in 1929?

T. C.: In 1929. I was at Duke from 1929 to 1931.

B. C.: That was a relatively brand new school at that time, wasn't it?

T. C.: It was brand new. They had granted only one Ph.D. when I arrived there. That was to Ralph Flanders, who spent all the rest of his academic life at New York University. Then came Robert Woody, who collaborated with Francis Simkins on a seminal book on reconstruction in South Carolina. They, as a matter of fact, set a new direction in the writing of reconstruction history and in reinterpreting of reconstruction.

B. C.: So you were one of the first persons to receive a Doctorate in History at Duke University?

T. C.: I was among the first four or five who got a doctorate.

B. C.: How did you like Duke?

T. C.: I was crazy about it. I was there in its disorganized years, but it was a vibrant place.

B. C.: But it had an old country southern charm about it, even when it was very new, didn't it?

T. C.: That is right. Well, my first year was actually spent in old Trinity College. My second year was out in all that mud and construction site for the new campus. If you go there now, you cannot visualize what a disorganized place it was in 1931.

They had a really good library then, and it has been greatly expanded.

B. C.: On what subject did you write your doctorate thesis?

T. C.: Well, I did my Master's thesis here in Kentucky on the subject that interested me then, and has interested me ever since--the trade between this section and the lower South in livestock, slaves, and hemp.

I went down to Duke with the intention of doing my doctoral dissertation on the development of the river trade along the Ohio and Mississippi rivers. But that was a pretty provincial place, and my major professor could not see over the Appalachian highlands. So he steered me onto a fairly interesting subject, but it became unexciting as time went on--the building of the southern railroads prior to the Civil War.

B. C.: You were at Duke when you met Elizabeth?

T. C.: Yes. She had graduated from Greenville Woman's College, now Furman University, and had gone to Simmons College in Boston and graduated there in Library Science. She was hired in that new Duke University library system. I met her--obviously graduate students are thrown in very close association with the library staff. Most of the time, however, graduate students are turned off by the library staff members.

B. C.: And when were you married?

T. C.: Our marriage was not what you would call a whirlwind affair. We became engaged in 1931, expecting to get married at Christmas or in the spring. The Depression hit the University of Kentucky hard and we put it off in 1931, expecting to get married in the spring of 1932. But things were worse by Christmas of 1932. By that time we were practically bankrupt here at the university. Finally, 1933 looked a little better. I went to see President Frank L. McVey and explained that I either had to tell Miss Turner that we were going to get married or tell her that we could not get married. He said, "Go ahead and get married. I think we'll be allright now." And I married her, took her away from a good-paying job in a good stable university.

A LAND OF CONTRAST

"**Kentucky has almost as many faces** as there are sectional divisions of the state. Whether it be the colonel with his goatee and julep or the mountaineer with his hog rifle and jug of moonshine, the image seldom, if ever, is an accurate one. Blazing a path into the heart of the first trans-Appalachian frontier, pioneer Kentuckians were apprentices to the westward movement along the western waters. Out of the stirring early years of international conflict, Indian wars, and pioneering, arose heroes like George Rogers Clark, Daniel Boone, Simon Kenton, Benjamin Logan, and Isaac Shelby. There were also rascals like James Wilkinson and the hired men. Behind the heroes were yeomen settlers who were less heroic in opening farms, building villages and towns, and opening the rich trade down river to the southern markets. The mixed reputations of the "Kentucks" were established both aboard flatboats drifting south and in the salons of plush steamboats as much as in the mountains, Bluegrass, and Pennyroyal.

The past supplies the Kentuckian a basis of comparison of his own condition and is a rich source of nostalgia. It would be difficult to imagine a people embraced by a single set of political boundaries who presented sharper contrasts than have Kentuckians. Sectional and social boundaries within the state have ever been separate influences."

B. C.: *What prompted you to come to Kentucky?*

T. C.: I am a graduate of the University of Mississippi. While I was a student there I was on the staff of the college newspaper. I have just been back to a reunion of that staff and I found out how poor we were in those days and how little news, really, was generated on that campus. I covered the chancellor's office and I got to know Chancellor Alfred Hume fairly well. One day during my junior year--I never had a senior year--I met him on the campus and he said, "I have just attended a meeting of southern university presidents and I met Dr. Frank L. McVey of the University of Kentucky. He asked me to have one of our boys make application for a scholarship at the university." I did, and got a little $200 scholarship. I came here not knowing a soul in Kentucky.

B. C.: What were your expectations of Kentucky before you came here?

T. C.: Almost as if I had been going into South Africa. I did not quite know what to expect. I had only a very superficial notion about the state. I knew about the feuds in the mountains and I had simply--like most people outside of Kentucky--translated those feuds into being typical of the whole state.

I had read John Fox, Jr.'s novels and also some of James Lane Allen. I had sort of a romantic notion of Kentucky. I knew about, in a vague way, the Bluegrass area, and I had some knowledge of the western part of the state. I had worked on a dredge boat for two years and the old captain on that boat, H. L. Lewis, was from Paducah. He used to sit and talk about his Kentucky days down in the Purchase area. He described the tobacco Black Patch War of that region. One of the things he said was that in the mornings after one of those raids he'd go out and pick up a whole nail keg full of horse shoes that had fallen off in the road from the horses. That was hard for me to believe. It still is.

I lacked a quarter's work to complete my degree at Ole Miss. The dean permitted me to do a very unusual thing. He allowed me to go to the University of Virginia and register for summer classes, a full quarter of work. I finished work actually for my A. B. at Virginia and transferred the credits back to Mississippi.

I came to Kentucky from Charlottesville, Virginia. I rode into Lexington not knowing what to expect and not having the slightest idea about the town. I got on the C & O train at Charlottesville the night before. There was a lot of excitement. People were running up and down the aisles all excited about something. A woman in the seat ahead of me with two little girls, from Louisville, asked, "Do you know who is on this train?" I had no idea who was on it. She said, "Chief Charlie Curtis, candidate for the vice-presidency on the Hoover ticket." He was in a rear coach and the people I saw running up and down the corridor were newspaper reporters going back to talk to the old Chief.

I asked the porter to get me up the next morning in time for Lexington and he got me up in Ashland, which as you realize was far more than ample time to get dressed to get off in Lexington. I jumped up, a country boy, got dressed in a hurry and came out of the berth and there was only one seat made up in the coach. There was this little roly-poly, bald-headed man sitting in that seat and he invited me to sit down by him. He was Charlie Curtis, and I rode into Lexington in the same seat with him.

B. C.: That would be about what date?

T. C.: That was September 14, 1928.

B. C.: Did you discuss national politics?

T. C.: Not much. We talked about what we were seeing along the way. I did ask him about his campaign. He said it was going well, which it was. We got down to Morehead and the porter came and said there were people out there who wanted the Chief to come out and make a speech. He patted me on the knee and said, "Son, just keep your seat. I'll go back there and make a little speech and come back." And he said, "This is a tough town."

Well, I did not know anything about Morehead. I had never heard of Morehead, Kentucky. While Chief Charlie

Curtis was making his speech, I sat and looked around at a "tough Kentucky town". Actually, it was the first place in Kentucky that I got a full, clear focus on.

Morehead, of all places.

Well, we rolled into Lexington, and I think every Republican in Kentucky was down at the old Union Station to meet us. I had great difficulty getting off of that train. I got into a taxicab and came out to the university to register.

B. C.: I suppose that was the last time you saw Charlie Curtis?

T. C.: The last I ever saw of him. That is quite true. The next thing I knew about Charlie Curtis, he was elected Vice-President of the United States and was in that terrific argument over his sister-in-law, Dolly Gann, and her position at the State dinners as his female escort.

B. C.: Mrs. Gann?

T. C.: Yes, you know, Dolly Gann. The issue was where she would be seated on State occasions and all that created quite a whoop-to-do. She was his sister-in-law. Charlie had no wife and she was his closest female relative.

B. C.: Where did he get the word "Chief"?

T. C.: He had some Indian blood in him.

B. C.: So, now you're here in Kentucky...

T. C.: Thousands and thousands of people had come to Kentucky, many of them from Virginia, just as I had done. Without my knowing it, I was making that same entry from Virginia, over the mountains into the state. Except I came on the C & O and they came over by river or over land through the Cumberland Gap.

B. C.: How old were you then?

T. C.: I was twenty-five years old. One of the first things I noticed was Kentuckians' deep affection for counties. And I think they attached certain English affections for localities. Certainly we, in Mississippi, did not emphasize counties as much as they do here in Kentucky. One of the first things I discovered was that they do not tell you they were from Eddyville. They would say they were from Lyon County. Or they did not say they were from Paris. They'd say "I'm from Bourbon County." I noticed that they were quick to tell you about the county. Kentuckians still are.

B. C.: Did you find that unique to Kentucky?

T. C.: Oh, I think Virginians still do a certain amount of it. And many Southerners do it. But Kentuckians emphasize it the most. I got so tired of answering the question, "Where were you born?" They were attaching such great importance to being born in Kentucky. My notion about it all is, that we all had to be born somewhere, and we had very little to do with where we were born. It did not make a bit of difference where you were born as to your academic and intellectual interests. That didn't have a thing to do with it. Intellectual interests are not congenital things. I became interested in Kentucky, and the reason I am still interested in it, is that it is a state of such sharp contrasts--so many different sections. People have reacted to environment, geography, to all sorts of influences differently in the different sections.

The second thing that interested me was the aura of romance that hangs over this state and it certainly trades off on that. For instance, in the first week of May it trades heavily on the Derby--the romance and excitement of the Derby. Well, those of us who live here know that it touches our lives very little. The Louisville businesses have got to make a year's profit in a week's time. This is good stock and trade. There is nothing wrong with that. We know that is essential.

I spent a lot of time trying to sort out the realities of Kentucky from the romantic concepts. I have a notion that Kentucky people--God knows they do it elsewhere--try to rationalize their shortcomings by romanticizing some of the things that are distinctive about their society. And they have done a pretty good job of that.

I soon became very interested in the relationship between Kentucky and the lower South. This relationship had an important bearing on this state during the Civil War. Of course, Kentucky developed some very intimate blood ties with the lower South, and it developed enormous economic ties with the region. Generally I think Kentuckians are southern oriented. Now, you take the people down in western Kentucky in the Pennyrile and Purchase areas--they are just as Southern as the people in Mississippi and Tennessee. They react the same way to things. But, there's a difference. Once you get up into this Bluegrass area, they are not quite that kind of Southerner. The differences are pretty subtle. It would be very difficult for me to be specific as to what the differences are.

I became interested in Kentucky's history right off and I have never lost that interest. After nearly 60 years, I've been up one side of the fence and down the other. I think I know most of the problems that Kentucky can have and I think that is because I have become very sympathetic with the continuing efforts to bring about changes. Certainly I would be lost if I undertook to go anywhere else to live. Because of the intimate ties, the emotional attachments, and the intellectual ties that I have in this state I would not want to go anywhere else.

B. C.: You raised the subject of counties. Why does Kentucky have so many?

T. C.: For various reasons. Georgia has more counties--I believe Texas has more--than Kentucky, and possibly so does California. But Kentucky is in the high county range. It stands about fourth or fifth in the nation on that score.

Now, as to the reason for these counties. There's a multiplicity of reasons. First of all is simply the creation of an old English system of local government. The magistrate, the county court, county sheriff, county clerk, and county constable, all of these we got directly from England. We have made some adaptations in local government, but basically the institution is English in origin. You take Fayette County, for instance. Fayette County and Kent County in England are almost blood cousins. You can hardly tell one from the other in many general respects. Both places feel the need for local government, are provincial, and land oriented.

There are several reasons for the many counties that are now apparent. One, was that deep feeling of a close human democratic association to government. As you know, Jefferson said it is much more important for a man to know his county official than to know who is the President of the United States. That says a lot. In order for an individual to have a direct say in government, the closer he gets to the local situation, the more clearly he can exercise a voice in making decisions. That's one reason.

The second reason is that this land system is a damnable one. It is of old English origin. I've undertaken several times to trace the land system as it exists here in Kentucky all the way back to its medieval beginnings. It goes all the way back to England and even to Norman France. I have never found a source that would give me a clear-cut notion about landholders and about the manner of surveying and boundary markings and the lawsuits that came up over land abroad. Well, in making a deed here in Kentucky, you can make a blunder that can invalidate the whole thing. It's very important that deed be registered at the court house. For a little fellow who came out and laid claim to 80 acres of land under the Kentucky metes and bounds survey system, or an irregular number of acres--he is not going to be careful enough with the deed, but if the place of registry was a long way off, he most likely was not going to register that deed. So, to protect it, he felt he had to have a county court house nearby--an easy muleback ride from his house to the county offices.

Another factor which is not often discussed is one I think might altogether be overlooked. In the settlement of this western country, there was a lot of violence. There was a lot of violence between the whites and Indians and that transferred over into violence among the whites. Disputes over landholdings, disputes over livestock, disputes over women, God knows what all--everything that human beings could get upset over prevailed here in Kentucky. That meant you had to have a constabulary force near at hand to control violence. Therefore you needed a county sheriff near at hand.

Now, those are some of the basic reasons for so many counties. In Littell's *Festoons of Fancy,* there is a little essay in which he states, "The reason we create a new county is there are so many rascals among us that we want to control the law enforcement officials." In that case, he is suggesting we want to be willing to violate the law at will and get by with it.

Then, geography plays a part in the forming of counties. So much of Kentucky is rocky, steep, and difficult to access--especially in eastern Kentucky. You have many counties that were simply formed within natural geographical boundaries.

We could reduce 120 counties to fewer than 60, if that many, and we possibly would not have a reduction of services. But I do not believe the people will ever eliminate a county. I believe that is impossible. However, modern Kentucky is rapidly coming to the point of merging a lot of public services. Jails, for instance, or public health units, and in some respects our educational systems, and all sorts of other welfare services. More and more things like the Department for Human Resources are lowering the old classical, provincial county boundaries.

Law enforcement now can no longer be confined within county boundaries. A criminal can commit an act and within ten-minutes be over a county boundary. So, more and more, the state police system is stepping in. And we have a lot of officials supporting the retention of expensive courthouses and supporting the public services centering around them and it costs us one whale of a lot of money.

Yet, there is a good amount of emotional sentiment in living in a county. For instance, Woodford County. Can you imagine erasing the Woodford and Fayette County boundaries? Could you imagine eliminating McCracken County or Graves County or Trigg County or Warren? Or going into eastern Kentucky in Pike or Harlan and erasing those boundaries? You would have a civil war on your hands. Yet, if you undertook to get those people to vote to increase taxes to support the services that they need inside their outmoded counties, they would buckle at that. The jails right now are presenting a real problem. More and more I see signs of merging services like that. We do hold onto our Old English traditions. That's where we go back to England, back to Virginia, and we go back to our own landlocked or provincial history.

B. C.: How much has the mother state of Virginia influenced Kentucky?

T. C.: I would say the overall concept of a way of life in Kentucky reflects, sometimes in pretty subtle form, its Virginia background. Such things as architectural forms reflect Virginia. The educational system in this state was for years bound by the old academy idea of Virginia. Many other areas, including the structure of local government, reflects the Virginia influence.

B. C.: *How did Kentucky acquire its existing boundaries?*

T. C.: I think I can explain most of that.

First place, would not it be wonderful if you could just wave a wand and remove everybody from Kentucky for 48 hours and then resurvey the land system in the state so that you have a north and south, east and west, rectilineal land survey? Would not that be marvelous if you could establish hard and fast boundary markers? You would starve a lot of lawyers to death. You would wreck a lot of legal history in this state. You might erase a lot of prominent Kentucky names if you did that.

The second thing, you look at the shape of Kentucky on a map and you wonder, "How in the name of God did people ever lay out a state like that?" This is not the only state in the Union that has crazy boundaries, but it is running right up at the top for queer geographical shape and queer specific boundaries. Now, there are a lot of reasons for that.

Number one is the river system. The Ohio and Mississippi Rivers obviously would establish boundaries of a fairly stable nature. The Big Sandy River in the east did the same thing. And it is a wonder that the Tennessee and Cumberland Rivers have not created more prominent boundaries. Those natural things such as rivers are pretty permanent.

Then, the topography of the western part of this Appalachian plateau played a big role in the shaping of the state. Of course, there are some arbitrary lines in the boundaries of Kentucky that were established by man. They make a little more sense. They have to conform, however, to the geographical natural boundaries.

Then man came along with the rivalry between England and the French in the French-Indian War, resulting in the Treaty of Paris in 1763. Virginia extended its boundaries to the Ohio River and beyond, actually, to the Mississippi River. In 1776, Virginia spread a blanket of authority over this western region without setting boundaries. It created Fincastle County. Fincastle County was simply a wave of the hand establishing a blanket of state authority. Then in 1776, it created Kentucky County and its boundaries took on a little more definite form. But even it was little more than a wave of the political hand. And then came 1780 and the establishment of the three original counties in Kentucky of Jefferson, Lincoln, and Fayette. Now Fayette was all north of the Kentucky River. From Benson's Creek at the Kentucky, a line was drawn down to the southern boundary of Kentucky. The territory west of the Benson's Creek boundary was Jefferson and to the east was Lincoln. Those were just three big, sprawling, general areas under the legal cover of counties. After the creation of those three counties, you began to have a fairly rapid immigration movement into the state and as you did so, the counties expanded in number. There were six counties when Kentucky became a state and in the history of Kentucky counties you will see a note "carved from Jefferson County", or "from Lincoln County", or "from Fayette County". That means those three old parcels were being carved into smaller governmental units. And that had something to do with the shape of the state and with the outer boundaries of Kentucky.

Then, around 1779, there was run between North Carolina Territory, which is now Tennessee, and Virginia Territory the so-called Walker Line. Felix Walker undertook a survey between the western territories. The Walker Line ostensively established most of the southern boundary between Kentucky and Tennessee but they fiddle-diddled with that for years. Over and over they surveyed parts of it. By 1860, the states of Tennessee and Kentucky were in conflict over that boundary. It is a complicated story, but there was a sliding arrangement that Kentucky could make public land grants inside the so-called Walker Survey Line for a limited number of years. I made an error in a book I wrote once without realizing it. I discovered where the Kentucky legislature had ceded land in Tennessee, once thinking that was some kind of curious phenomenon. Well, it was not. It was perfectly legal but I did not know it at the time.

In 1860, the two states came to grips with this problem over boundaries. They recorded what was known as the "Cox-Peebles Survey". The new survey started at the New Madrid Bend and established a big stone corner marker at the western extremity. The surveyors cut off that small tip of Kentucky where you have to go through Tennessee or Missouri or down the river to reach it. You cannot get to it directly from Kentucky. Every five miles from the base marker to the east side of the Cumberland Gap, stone markers were placed, marking the boundary between the two states. The "Cox-Peebles Survey" settled the dispute between Kentucky and Tennessee.

There were two or three very interesting things in that battle. One was the Black-Jack Jog which is in Simpson County. The center of the Jog is in the middle of Highway 31W that jumps down and then comes back into a small "V" shape on the southern boundary. Just east of that is another jog which is square-cut. I believe that's called the "Middleton Jog". That one was political. The Black-Jack Jog was simply the result of a cloudy day and the surveyors were off in the readings of the compass. There is a legend they were drunk.

In 1799, Kentucky and Virginia settled the boundaries between their two states. Surveyors started at the Cumberland Gap and went up the spine of Pine Mountain all the way to above Harlan County to a point near the forks of the Elkhorn. There they set a straight-line on a reading of the compass and surveyed a line up to the middle fork of the Big Sandy. Then they surveyed down the Big Sandy all the way to the Ohio. That established the eastern and southeastern boundaries of the state.

In 1818, there was added to the state those counties in the Jackson Purchase Area. That required some surveying from the Tennessee River to the New Madrid Bend and Reelfoot Lake and across it. The boundary along the northwestern part of the state and the Ohio River was in jeopardy. Over and over this has been in jeopardy. Finally, as you know, it's just now being settled by a Federal Commission. Kentucky now has ownership to an arbitrary line adjoining Indiana and Ohio and following the Ohio River. Nobody can possibly say where the low-water mark was at any time, certainly not in 1789. At last the boundary lines of Kentucky are being settled. That does not mitigate the fact that Kentucky is a very curiously shaped state. Irvin Cobb said whimsically that it reminded him of a camel trying to get up. Well, that's referring to that humped-up section of the Bluegrass Plateau.

B. C.: Why is the Tennessee boundary with the Jackson Purchase farther south than the rest of the state?

T. C.: The boundary line between the Tennessee and Cumberland Rivers has a jog at a diagonal that extends down in the land between the lakes. There were people living in that area by the time that boundary was established for the Purchase. Some of them wanted to live in Kentucky and used some political pressure. That is how that came into being.

B. C.: It seems that at an early time in Kentucky history--the time of Henry Clay, the Breckinridges, Crittendens, and the Stevensons--Kentucky played a more prominent and influential role in national affairs than it has since the Civil War.

T. C.: There are a lot of facts involved. You see, this was the first frontier state created. It was literally carved out of the western frontier. There was a heavy population movement into this western country into the Ohio Valley, Kentucky, and eventually across into the Indiana, Illinois, and Missouri territories and on to the other states.

Kentucky attracted a large number of lawyers. Many of them came because of the land situation. I do not know whether that was the only reason or not, but that was one. As you know, Kentucky has always had a strong legal tradition. Well, when you have lawyers, you are going to have politicians. Many lawyers find it attractive to get into politics, and many of them find that necessary to make a living. By 1800, the migration had moved some important figures into the state. In the early period there was George Nicholas, who was called "The Father of the Constitution of Kentucky". There was Caleb Wallace, George Robertson, John Breckinridge, and others who became important figures in this country. They were men who stood out from the crowd. I think they would have anywhere, certainly in this western country and certainly in Congress and national politics.

Then in 1797 along comes Henry Clay, a young man who became a spokesman for the west after 1800. That was a very significant time in Kentucky history--from 1790 up to 1850. If I were going to pick out a period that brought Kentucky to its greatest potential and expansion in many fields, that 60 year period would be the one that I would pick. Kentucky expanded rapidly population-wise, economically, politically, and socially. Kentucky had a real impact on western trade and on the political affairs that pertained to the western expansion.

In getting themselves elected to office and keeping themselves in office, these men of substance were able to exert more than just the usual individual political influence.

Then there was the matter of catering to the rising

western vote. The west was becoming more and more an area to be reckoned with in national politics. No longer was it an east of the mountains or an Atlantic coastal situation. This new west was becoming a growing force.

There was also the matter of international issues and the control of the navigation on the waters of the Mississippi River by either the United States or Spain or France. One of the major events in Kentucky history was the Louisiana Purchase. It brought along a tremendous amount of adjustments in internal affairs. Also, there was that rising period of intense national issues with the West becoming increasingly nationalistic. This was a growing place with youthful leadership. Clay stepped right into that role. As the issues with England became more unsettled and the War of 1812 approached, Clay was a young war-hawk, not only in Kentucky, but nationally. He was the voice of westward expansion. As you know, he got himself elected Speaker of the House in his first appearance in Congress. Then, of course, other Kentucky leaders came along who were to play an important role. You jump from Clay to Crittenden. There were a lot of Kentucky leaders in between those two who were to exert substantial national political influence. Take Richard M. Johnson, for instance, over at Georgetown, who became a Jacksonian. John Adair is another one--a big Jacksonian. You can go on down the list to Charles Morehead. You can pick out a lot of names that stood out from the crowd, like Joseph Hamilton Daviess. They might not stand out so much from the crowd today, but this was a place where the crowd wasn't as large and it was easier to make a mark.

Then, Kentuckians exerted a lot of influence on national appointments. Kentucky was to have an inordinate number of people appointed--territorial judges, clerks, other court officials, governors, Secretary of State, the secretaries of territories. There was a period of unusual expansion for Kentucky.

By 1850, you see this influence begin to sag.

That was Kentucky's period. It never reclaimed its national position in leadership after the death of John J. Crittenden and John C. Breckinridge.

B. C.: Did the decline of Kentucky in national influence have any relationship at all with the fact that it was a southern state that did not secede, yet was treated afterwards as a southern state that had seceded? Did we lose our national prominence because of our failure to take a strong stand--as a state--one way or the other during the Civil War?

T. C.: That's a complex question. There are a lot of intricate issues related to Kentucky's position during the Civil War.

B. C.: You regard the Louisiana Purchase as being one of the watershed events in Kentucky history. Name another one.

T. C.: This is right off the top of my head. One thing that I think hit this state just like a cannonball right in the middle was the Goebel affair. It was, as I said in *Kentucky, Land of Contrasts,* this state's darkest hour. We spent years getting over that. It was not only a matter of the murder of a man, but it was also the murder of honor and humanity of the Commonwealth.

B. C.: Concerning the assassination of William Goebel, which had the greatest impact--the assassination of Goebel or the stealing of that election?

T. C.: Why, to the decency and integrity of the Commonwealth, it was the stealing of the election. That would have to be put first. The stealing of the election was corrupt and disruptive. It besmirched the whole integrity of the democratic system.

B. C.: What about William Goebel as a man? For a governor and political leader who was assassinated, he has not been immortalized.

T. C.: No, he was not a loveable character. There were people who supported Goebel, like the Populists, the dissatisfied, the politically dislocated, and the people who were fed up with the corporate control and management of this state. Many voted for William Goebel because he was the only chance they had to get away from what had been going on in Kentucky politics for the last quarter of a century. Everything bad had gone on. Kentuckians being what they are, and I think I understand their personality, they would not have voted for Goebel as a human being. He was the only choice they had. Either that or the Republican Taylor, and they did not like that choice either.

B. C.: Of course, history pretty well confirms now that Taylor did in fact win the election.

T. C.: I do not think there is much doubt about it. Everything that I have read indicates pretty clearly that Taylor won the election.

I intended, but never did get around to it, to go and talk to Jim Howard before he died.

B. C.: Who was Jim Howard?

T. C.: Jim Howard was the man who was sent to the penitentiary for killing Goebel. Caleb Powers did not kill him and Henry Youtsey, I think, pretty clearly did not kill him. Jim Howard, no doubt, was the man who was best situated to kill him, but nobody knows, to this day, positively who killed him. It was an assassination associated with that election. There's no question about that. They knew that things were in such an emotional state in Frankfort, and the Republicans knew that the Democratic legislature was going to throw out the election results. It would be hard for me to believe that the Republican Party as a whole would subscribe to murder in that case. Jim Howard was convicted but there was no witness who could point a finger and say, "That is the man who fired the gun." The gun was shot from the Secretary of State's office, there on the second floor of the old Capitol Annex office building. I did interview the man who got into that room first after the shooting. There was smoke in the room and there was a gun in the room which I think is in Frankfort somewhere right now. There was nobody in the room.

Let's go back to your question about watershed events. There was an incident that occurred here in Kentucky that had important bearings, I think, and those were the great revivals at the turn of the nineteenth century. The establishment of revival meetings and outpouring of emotions--it almost marked a psychological moment in state development. This was not a statewide event, but it nevertheless played an important role.

One of the most fortunate things that ever happened in Kentucky was the fact that the Civil War did not spill over any more than it did into this state. The Civil War actually resulted in very little damage to the state aside from the L & N Railroad. You had no real battles fought in populated areas that destroyed towns and cities or civilian life. The fact that the major Civil War battles pretty much bypassed Kentucky was a very fortunate thing. If the Confederates had invaded Kentucky with impelling force, they would have been able to establish that line they drew up from the Cumberland Gap all the way over to Columbus and the Mississippi River. If they could have established that line and held it, the Northern army would have moved into the state, and they would have fought some of the major battles of the war here. There would have been a tremendous cost to this state. I consider the fact that the Civil War bypassed Kentucky as being well worth serious and major consideration.

B. C.: What myths or distortions do you feel have come about in regards to Kentucky's role in the Civil War?

T. C.: Of course, there was a lot of romantic bravado in the early outbreak of the war. For example, the organization of the John Hunt Morgan command, which was a very flamboyant part of the war in the western Confederacy. That was just the kind of thing that would appeal to young Kentuckians who were able to ride away on horses and fight on horseback. Riding back and forth into Kentucky on the various Morgan raids was high drama stuff. That was exciting. What they accomplished may be another matter in the long-range of the history of the War. I doubt that they accomplished anything of major lasting importance, so Morgan's role may be a historical distortion. But they did bring the war home momentarily, and on sporadic occasions, to the people. I think it would not be unfair or unhistorical to say that Morgan's raids in Kentucky were more the stuff of what legends are made than of what actual military accomplishments were made. Certainly I have no intention of subtracting the raids of Morgan or the raids of the Orphan Brigade--any of those things were dramatic and exemplified the personal aspects of the war. I think, in a much less flamboyant way, the guerilla warfare that took place here in Kentucky, both in eastern and western Kentucky, was an unsettling thing.

Of course, the guerilla warfare was a covert affair. In a conventional war you knew who your enemies were and you knew who your friends were. There were no sides with the guerillas. They were enemies of everybody. I had some time on one occasion in Pike County and I thought I would like to see what was going on in this far eastern county during the Civil War. I looked through the court records. Those cases ran on down through the 1870's and there is some tremendously interesting material about the guerilla warfare. One cause of the famous McCoy-Hatfield feud and the fight that went on up there stemmed from guerilla activities. There was a strong element of that in that feud. Even in western Kentucky, you did not know who was who in the latter part of the war.

As to the wisdom of Kentucky's attempt to remain neutral during the war, if I had been living in Kentucky and voting in the General Assembly, I would have voted to remain neutral, too.

In that period between 1860 and 1861, Kentucky had everything to lose and nothing to gain by getting into the war. If the state had seceded, or if it had come out strong for the Union, it would have become a battleground immediately. Either way, it was damned. By taking a neutral course, Kentucky hoped to buy some time, or that is the way I read the arguments that were presented, to get people calmed down and to see which direction things were going. There were some shrewd people who could see what was going to happen. George D. Prentice of the *Louisville Journal*, was one of those people. There were members of the legislature who saw that if Kentucky ran headlong into taking sides it would be like putting its neck on a chopping block. And it would have been, in my opinion.

As you know, there's been an argument about who first invaded Kentucky--the Confederate or Union forces. I do not think there's any doubt that the Confederacy invaded Kentucky first. Had I been among the Confederate leadership, I would have wanted to invade Kentucky because it was vital to the Confederate scheme of things. Think of what was involved there--the L & N Railroad, the control of the Ohio River, the possible jumping off point to invading the Midwest. There was the possibility of drawing the Midwest into the support of the Southern cause. There were all sorts of complex issues involved if that could have been brought off. But that was an impossible dream. It did not happen that way.

Abraham Lincoln said the Union had to have Kentucky, almost at any cost. It could not afford to lose this state. Issuance of the "Lincoln guns" was a subtle way of invading Kentucky without doing so with troops under the flag. The War Department supplied guns to loyal Unionists who would support the state. Those guns were brought to Louisville, Maysville, and Lexington and taken to Camp Nelson for the purpose of outfitting the loyal Kentucky Unionists.

Again, going back to the subject of Kentucky neutrality, it was fortunate that the Confederates never could establish the anchorage line from Columbus to the Cumberland Gap. As you know, there were certain outbreaks along the line. There was that skirmish at Bowling Green. Johnson falling back from Bowling Green, went down by way of Dover, Tennessee, and wound up around Shiloh. There was the battle of the Wildcat, which was in Laurel County, and there was the battle of Mills Springs. But the Confederacy never could establish their line solidly in this area. That's one of the "ifs". If the Confederacy had been able to establish that line it might have done very much better in the affairs here in Kentucky.

I would like to sit down and trace out the lines of development in that cardinal moment that George D. Prentice and other individuals mapped out a procedure for the state early in 1861. It was fortunate that the legislature was not in session at that time. That gave Kentucky breathing room. That declaration of neutrality gave enough delay to prevent Kentucky from becoming a disastrous battlefield. Later on Kentucky was invaded by the Union and was badly mistreated. The Battle of Perryville, for all intents and purposes, wound up the major fighting so far as Kentucky was concerned. The rest of the campaigning consisted only of skirmishes.

Then you begin to have the setting up of temporary military units in command. One classic example was Thomas Palmer undertaking to free the slaves in Kentucky, and the concentration of freedmen at Camp Nelson. That is a tremendously interesting story of the attempt to wipe out slavery through that Camp Nelson concentration--first of the black soldiers, then of their families, and then of the non-military slaves seeking freedom. There has been published a book that contains the records of John G. Fee and other missionary activities at Camp Nelson in Garrard County during the ex-slave crisis.

B. C.: Where was Camp Nelson?

T. C.: This camp was near the Kentucky River. Camp Nelson itself was over about 6 or 7 miles from the Kentucky River but there was part of the Camp Nelson military concentration around the bridge crossing the Kentucky River itself.

Camp Nelson was a Northern stronghold. It and Dick Robertson were places to which the Lincoln guns were delivered. I own letters that were addressed to Congressman Robert Mallory, and one of them is addressed to Lincoln's first Secretary of War, Simon Cameron, saying that the time had come to send the Lincoln guns to Kentucky. These were dispatched to Maysville through Louisville and transported to Dick Robertson by way of Lexington.

B. C.: One of the great paradoxes of the Civil War in Kentucky was the fact that both Jefferson Davis and Abraham Lincoln were born within 90 miles of each other and their families emigrated and went in opposite directions; that Lincoln married a Lexington girl and Davis went to school there at Transylvania. In your studies of Kentucky history, have you discovered whether these two men ever crossed paths personally or did they have mutual friends?

T. C.: Well, quite frankly, I cannot answer whether or not they ever met. I would have to go back and check, but I do not recall seeing in any of the biographies of Lincoln whether he ever met Davis. Nor do I recall in the biography of Davis that he ever met Lincoln. I do not know whether Lincoln and Davis ever saw each other. If so, I would say that any contact they had would have to be of minor historical consequence, compared with the big issues involved.

Let us go back to their births. I suppose the Lincolns were poorer people than the Davises. But, I think when you say that, you are only saying something of degree, rather than something of dramatic difference. They were pretty much of the same yeoman farmer background. Davis was born in Fairview in relatively fertile farming country as compared with the poor ridge land around Hodgenville in LaRue County. The Davises were much better off, but that's only a relative matter. The significant factor there is that the Lincolns went directly westward in the frontier movement. They crossed the Ohio River into Indiana and from there went on into Illinois. And they came into contact with forces and points of view that were not prevalent in the South. As far as any southern Indiana influence was concerned, it was conservative. I think that same thing was largely true in Illinois.

Davis followed the other line of emigration, down the river to the lower South, and there became involved in the old cotton-slave system. Both the economy and the social systems were of a special nature. Davis came under that influence largely through his brother. Then, an important influence on Davis was that of being a frontier military officer in the Black Hawk and Mexican Wars. Next, was his rise to political office and political influence. Davis became a spokesman of that ultra-conservative southern group--pro slavery, pro cotton--southern rights group. He was not an extremist like many of his fellow southerners which included William L. Yancy or Edmund Ruffin. Davis was not an extremist, but he was clearly inside the southern planter political leadership category of that time.

What I am saying here is not so much concerned with Davis the politician getting into that situation as Secretary of War and as a member of the United States Senate; I am thinking that when Davis' family turned south, they turned their faces into an altogether different social and economic situation. Their points of view changed. They might not have been any different from the Lincolns here in Kentucky. Lincoln was always clear of the pro-southern situation. Lincoln's marriage to Mary Todd from Lexington no doubt introduced him to the central Kentucky politics and way of life. This, however, had limited bearing on him. I am not prepared to say how much, but he came here and visited with the Todds. He was mixed up here in the Bluegrass in two legal cases that had somewhat to do with slavery. A point is made by William Townsend in his book, *Lincoln In His Wife's Home Town* and by the other Lincoln biographies which told of his seeing slavery in central Kentucky. He had seen slavery on his flatboat trip to New Orleans and he knew a great deal about slavery early in his life. He had seen it firsthand, including the sale of slaves. He later witnessed the slave sales here in central Kentucky. By the 1840's and the Mexican War, Lincoln had become a Whig, and much later on he turned Republican. Lincoln and Davis were both politicians. They represented the points of view of their constituents. They represented their sections and attitudes of the times. Their points of origin, being born on Kentucky soil, had almost nothing to do with their later careers. It is interesting that the two men were born here, very much under the same circumstances. It is interesting that they rose to such high positions from the same background, but arrived at the peak of their careers by different routes. I think you could say that there was a lot of the Kentucky mind, from 1860 to 1865, that would not have varied from Lincoln's thinking or point of view. I think Lincoln, under certain circumstances, might have made some major compromises in order to preserve the Union, but he did not have the opportunity to do so. Davis, on the other hand, might have been much more reluctant to take extreme actions had he actually found himself in a situation to do that. That's just an observation. The two men faced enormous challenges and Davis lost. Lincoln proved, on the whole, to be a better administrator and a better political leader than Davis. They were different in fundamental political and administrative approaches.

B. C.: There has been a duelling tradition in Kentucky and there is a provision in the Kentucky Constitution prohibiting office-holders from being involved in duels. How exactly did that get into the Constitution?

T. C.: Kentuckians brought here from Virginia and elsewhere various policies and negative things in their way of life. One of those things, and I don't know where it originated--it goes back to England and France and Spain--a genuine sensitivity about honor. In the 1820's, 1830's, and 1840's especially, honor became a very highly revered thing here in Kentucky and the South. Henry Clay fought a duel with Humphrey Marshall when he was in the Kentucky legislature. He also fought one with John Randolph of Roanoke. Then there was the Trotter-Metcalfe duel. Trotter was an editor of a newspaper here in Lexington. That attracted a lot of attention. There were other duels in Kentucky in various places. Duelling became the mark of the gentleman defending his honor, such honor as he had.

By the late 1840's there were enough duels and enough deaths or serious injuries that it attracted an enraged public attention. When the delegates to the Constitutional Convention met in 1849, Ira Root, a delegate from Campbell County in northern Kentucky, introduced a resolution adding a section in the Constitution forbidding duelling, and that all elected officials be required to take an oath that they had not fought a duel. This resolution was discussed right extensively on at least two occasions before it was finally adopted. It appeared in the constitution requiring all incoming elected public officials to swear that he or she had not fought a duel, carried a challenge to a duel, or served as a second in a duel anywhere. That was adopted in both the third and fourth constitutions. It does not mean anything anymore. As far as I know, nobody's fighting a duel in Kentucky or has any intention of fighting one. Nevertheless, it is an active part of the Constitution. It seems silly. It is silly in this modern day.

B. C.: Do you know whether that provision is unique to the Kentucky Constitution or does it exist in any other state constitution in the United States?

T. C.: If there is a clause against duelling in any other constitution, I do not know about it. Or if it is required as an oath for the holding of an office, I don't know about it. I would doubt very seriously that it is. I think it is safe to say that Kentucky is the only state that has such a requirement.

It has been misread and a lot of fun has been poked at Kentucky over this portion of its constitution, when there are so many more things that public officials can do that would be of greater harm to the Commonwealth than fighting a duel. I am certainly not advocating fighting a duel by removing the oath, but that is an outmoded thing.

B. C.: What about the notoriety of the feuds in the eastern Kentucky mountains? What caused the feuds and have they been blown out of proportion as far as Kentucky's image is concerned?

T. C.: You've asked me at least a three-part question.

First, did the feuds damage Kentucky? Yes, sir. Seriously. During the late 1890's and the first decade of this century we had the outbreak of the Tolliver-Martin Feud, the Hargis-Cockerel Feud, the Talt-Hall war, the Hatfield-McCoy, and Baker versus White. You can continue with other family feuds, killings, and murders. Yes, sir. They damaged

Kentucky badly because the outside national press picked these things up and made Kentucky appear to be an unsafe state to visit. And also a state full of barbarians that should not be running loose. Finally, they made Kentucky appear to be tolerating murder while doing too little about it.

The cause of the feuds were many. Heaven knows if anyone could actually define all the causes of feuds. That old story about a pig causing the Hatfield-McCoy feud is myth to a large extent. I suppose there was a pig involved in it but the initial cause was the guerilla warfare and the choosing of sides during the Civil War. The court records of Pike County show pretty clearly that was an opening cause of the Hatfield-McCoy dispute.

Then there were women. That is always a sensitive issue. In the Hatfield-McCoy feud there was a woman issue involved.

B. C.: How was the woman issue involved in it?

T. C.: Marriage between families and the objections on the part of one family to the marriage.

B. C.: How extensive were the feuds in eastern Kentucky as opposed to what they have been built up to be?

T. C.: I think all the joking and all the humor about feuding and all the poems, jingles, and other writings about the feuds, and in recent years the hillbilly stuff that has appeared about Kentucky--I think is largely myth. People are quick to say that the good folks did not do those things, and that is true. But the trouble about the people who engaged in those sort of things, they weren't the "good" people. They were largely a violent, illiterate class of people. The good people were afraid to do anything much to put down the feuds.

Another major cause of feuding was that country people living in isolated areas can become terribly sensitive, not over big things, but over the least little irritating social affair. Some kind of imagined slight, some kind of encroachment, or some kind of dispute over a land line, a horse trade, dog or gun trade could start a war. There are a thousand and one things, sometimes so miniscule that nobody would think about which would cause rural violence. These can grow into a terrifically important thing. Kentucky has had more than its share of publicity about the feuds, and had the state gone on as it was headed in those decades of 1890 to 1910, it no doubt would have gone to pieces in the breakdown of law and order.

The governors had their hands full, of course, in the Black Patch War. It took a lot of courage, a lot of action and a lot of planning to put down that kind of strife. And it was hard to put down a feud in the mountains because you did not know who was in it, or who was who as to sides. You did not know what the grapevine was transmitting about the official presence. It was not an easy matter to work with.

B. C.: You were talking about the lasting effect that the Goebel assassination had on Kentucky's reluctance to accept change, and that being unsettling. The Constitution of 1890 also restricted the constitutional officers such as governor and others from succeeding themselves. What gave rise to that provision?

T. C.: I think that the answer to that question lies in the fear that a governor, for instance, would get into office and simply build up a "machine" and keep himself in office, maybe even becoming an imperial governor because you could not get him out. He could build a "machine" that would keep him in power. Whereas, if he was going out of power every four years, he would lose the political machine that he had built up and the influence that he had established. I suppose there is a certain amount of Jacksonian philosophy that offices ought to be handed around. Rotation of public office is a very healthy thing. That early political attitude played a part in it.

B. C.: Why does Kentucky, a state so steeped with Indian folklore, have so few towns with Indian names?

T. C.: I think there are several reasons why that's true.

First, the great amount of Indian culture, the artifacts, which are found in this state are not really the "red" Indian artifacts, as I understand, but they are from the prehistoric stone-age Indians. That simply means that they did not establish towns. If they did, you do not know much about them. All you know is you find some deposits of kitchen middens or chippings or other evidence of cliff houses or mounds where they lived. You do not find any great concentration, or any names. The only Indian name that I know that goes back any distance is Eskipakathiki, an old Shawnee trading post in Clark County. Down in western Kentucky, you have Kuttawa, which is an Indian name and Paducah, which is also an Indian name.

On the other hand, in Mississippi, you had a very mature Indian civilization planted there. They had Indian towns, streams, and the white man came along and adopted their names for counties. For instance, I was born near the Tallahega Creek, near Mashualaville. There were other places which the Indians named, like Natchez, and Tallahatchie. You can go on with an endless trail of names.

Those Indians were right there in named communities. They were removed, most of them were, by the terms of the Dancing Rabbit Treaty.

B. C.: What was the Dancing Rabbit Treaty?

T. C.: That was a transfer of the Choctaw holdings in the South to the United States Government in exchange for land in the Oklahoma Indian territory.

Here in Kentucky, you have one Indian remains--the Old Warriors Trace. When I say remains, I mean you can locate various segments of it. But, that is about the only road that I know that bore an Indian name. It is hard to distinguish between an Indian trail and a buffalo trace.

There were no red Indians to amount to anything who ever established a stronghold in Kentucky. There were Indians like those around Paducah, and the Cumberland and Tennessee Rivers. But throughout Kentucky, generally, you do not have any sites of Indian towns. The Shawnee came in here from the north with the Delawares, the

Wyandots, and all the associated northern tribes. From the south came the Cherokees, but they never remained here. They hunted here and they did some trading here but they never lingered to establish an Indian civilization. The Chickasaws owned the Purchase Area, but they certainly never lived there on a permanent basis. They were there just then for a very brief period of time. They all lived in northern central Mississippi. That is one reason why Andrew Jackson and Isaac Shelby were able to buy the Jackson Purchase Area from the Chickasaws. To them it was surplus land that they weren't using.

As I said before, there are artifacts scattered all over this state. I do not suppose there is a place you can go that you do not come upon artifacts. There are literally thousands of them. Many of those belonged to the pre-historic Indians.

I don't pretend to be an Indian archeologist, but I do know that you did not have the permanent settlements. Around the mountains, you will find all kinds of evidence of the cliff-dwellers. They lived at the cliff-line but they evidently hunted and gathered fruit in the valleys. I do not know much about those people.

Prehistoric Kentucky is exciting. You don't have much evidence to go on, other than artifacts, and a lot of that you have to more or less guess at their use or make common sense guesses.

I've been trying to think how many Kentucky counties have Indian names and Ohio County is the only one I can think of. I believe it is the only county that has an Indian name.

In all of the discussion about the meaning of the name of Kentucky, I think somewhere in the neighborhood of "Great Meadowland" has some justification. The name of the state itself comes from the river, but where did the Kentucky River name come from? How did that originate? It seems to me that "Great Meadowland" would have a reasonable natural foundation. In Kerr's *History of Kentucky, Volume I,* there is quite a bit of discussion about the Indian origin of the name.

B. C.: How did the term "dark and bloody ground" become attached to Kentucky?

T. C.: That originated with Chief Dragging Canoe at the

Treaty of Sycamore Shoals in 1775.

B. C.: How did that arise?

T. C.: When Richard Henderson, the Harts, and other members of the Transylvania Company negotiated the Treaty of Sycamore Shoals, they received the land south of the Kentucky River for the Transylvania Company. There were some young Cherokee chiefs who were badly dissatisfied with that treaty. One, Dragging Canoe, told Henderson, "You have bought a noble bargain", and said to the effect, "It will become a dark and bloody ground." That prophecy proved true; it did become a dark and bloody ground. Daniel Boone lost a son at Cumberland Gap in a Cherokee raid on an emigrating party.

There may be other names that you will see mentioned every once in awhile but I think that the "Great Meadowland" comes pretty close to being acceptable.

B. C.: And that came from the Kentucky River--Kentucky got its name from the Kentucky River?

T. C.: Yes, the Kentucky River. It might be that the Kentucky River itself is a derivative of Iroquois. They had, at one time, asserted a claim to this country.

It was an Indian name to start with, and the land of Kentucky simply was derived from the river, Kentucky. It is a pretty name. It has been Anglicized, that is pretty obvious. It would have had to have been Anglicized. Kentucky is one of the pretty Indian names in the nomenclature of the American states. Others are Ohio, Tennessee, Mississippi, Iowa, Wisconsin, Indiana and Illinois.

B. C.: You talk about the distinct regions of Kentucky in your book, "Kentucky, Land of Contrast", to a great extent.

T. C.: I am very interested in the sectional aspects of Kentucky. About a month ago, a group meeting in Ashland had as their theme, "What Unites Us and What Divides Us", and I began thinking about that as a topic of pretty vital importance to the state. There are a lot of physical forces which divide its people, and against the unified state as a whole. It is extremely difficult to write about Kentucky. No novelist has ever written "the" Kentucky novel. It is hard to draw all of Kentucky into a history of the state. Luckily, the historian can do something that the novelist cannot do. He can treat topics topographically in a book. In writing about any aspect of Kentucky, you have to be thoroughly conscious of the sectional influence and geographical forces that are constantly at work. What are some of the forces that divide Kentucky? What are some of the geographical influences? We begin in the old part of the state that fought off penetration--the eastern highlands, the Appalachian Range, the Appalachian frontier of Kentucky on the east. That region ordinarily belongs geographically, topographically, economically--or measured by any other category or any standard--to eastern Tennessee, western Virginia, and western North Carolina and West Virginia. It belongs, really, in a state of Appalachia. I have never been one to believe in over emphasizing the sort of thing that used to be said more often than it is said now about a "pure Anglo-Saxon population". That implies those people poured into hollows and ravines and remained untouched by outside influences. There's much truth in that. I, however, used to get pretty tired of hearing people talk about speaking "pure Anglo-Saxon". There are a lot of words in use that were of ancient origins. There were a lot of expressions and maybe a lot of folkways that go back to the early English, Welsh, Irish and Scotch backgrounds, with some German influence thrown in for good measure. But eastern Kentucky is a land set apart and measured in many ways separately in state statistics. It is the area of Kentucky which has possessed the greatest amounts of resources--oil, coal, gas, water, and timber, and I suppose you could include stone in that, and maybe some other types of resources. It has been a land rich in these basic natural materials as compared with other parts of the state. Yet, in human terms, it has been a poorer land. It has been a land that has produced almost a congenital poverty level, a subsistence level would be a more reasonable term. It consisted of the small subsistence farmer, the small county seat towns, inadequate educational facilities, inadequate roads, institutions of every sort--hospitals, or you might even include the churches, the religious institutions. It is an area that has colleges in it, but the colleges in Appalachia have had too small an impact measured by the larger terms of the influences that colleges and universities should have on a section. It has been a land that has been open to exploitation by extraregional capital. That is, speculators in land, minerals, oil and gas who moved in and invested in cheap oil, timber, and coal lands and drained away a rich resource bounty. They have exploited the resources, but the capital from those has gone almost entirely outside the region to be spent. I think it would be amazing to Kentucky's people if they knew how much of Kentucky origin--how much money from Kentucky resources--has gone into the establishment and support of sophisticated institutions in the eastern United States, for instance, or in the mid-west. I think it would be a shocking revelation.

In the statistical tables--we will take the elementary one of agriculture--you do not begin to strike much of a rise in agricultural production until you get outside of the Appalachian counties. They have been populated by small farmers--subsistence farmers depending on the land for the bare necessities of human existence. They have been dependent on the rest of the state in many areas for leadership. They have often resisted change and have been extremely sensitive about criticism. Appalachian Kentucky is a region of extremely sensitive people. Though the region often has been strife-torn historically with the old blood feuds, there lingers on a sensitive regional defensiveness. Aside from the blood feuds, it has been a land of violence. There is a very bright young man, Robert Ireland, Professor of History at the University of Kentucky, who is now writing a book that should have been written a long time ago on the history of violence in Kentucky. Appalachia has had more than its share of violent times.

The political system in Kentucky is--I don't like to use the word "unique", and I'm not using that word here, but it has been pretty special--pretty distinctive of the region of eastern

Kentucky. There is no doubt about it, that as an independent region, Appalachia means a lot of things. It means a geographical region, a sociological region, a cultural region, and a resource region. Under the term "Appalachia" you have a broad spectrum of meaning and of human adaptation, progress and attitudes towards things. As I said earlier, you see it in John Fox's writing, in books by Harriette Arnow, Jesse Stuart, James Still, Harry Caudill, and other persons who have written about Appalachia.

Then, you come into this Bluegrass region. If you could take a knife and run it around the outer Bluegrass, the inner Bluegrass would have to sustain it and support it. And if you just depended on the central Kentucky region to make a statistical showing, it would make a favorable standing comparatively speaking with the rest of the nation. There you have had fertile land and the development of towns and cities. There you've had a development of outside trade right from the start going back to the earliest period of Kentucky history with that downriver trade, that rich agricultural livestock and crop development.

In the Pennyrile area of Kentucky you come into another region that has subtle differences, but sometimes at that not so subtle. The land is a highly sectionalized part of the state within the region itself. Not all of the Pennyrile is alike. There has been both a subsistence farming area, highly rural, with a rural state of mind, and reactions to politics, to institutional development, education, and anything else which denotes a change in the social and economic structure. Yet, it has been rich in resources. It has had the oil and gas, water and timber, and in large areas it has had a fertile soil, producing rich agricultural crops. You have had, historically, a distinct difference in the agricultural structure. Dark tobacco, for instance, was symbolic at one time of the region's economy and as you so well know, resulted in social and political chaos in the revolt against the discriminations and pressures that developed.

The Purchase Area is almost a region set apart by geography and politics. It wasn't added to the state until the other sections were mature and historically defined. I get the feeling, when I go into the Purchase region, that I am not quite in Kentucky. Many times I have felt in that area that I was more in the kindred area of west Tennessee. There, people are under the influence of Memphis or more nearly under the influence of St. Louis than Louisville and Lexington and I think they are.

Lying along the Ohio River frontier, or the northern Kentucky areas, the Ohio River Flood Plain is a distinct geographical region and a state of mind. Northern Kentucky is a very extremely sensitive region. It is sensitive, I think with some degree of guilt mixed in. It is obviously intimately tied up with southern Ohio and Cincinnati. Cincinnati has historically wielded an enormous influence on northern Kentucky. Yet, northern Kentucky struggles hard to be a functioning intimate and organic part of the state, complaining at times of discrimination on the part of the General Assembly and some institutions in the state. The funding of Northern Kentucky University, for instance, is indicative of this fact.

Then you have the development of the big urban center, Louisville, on the Ohio River at the falls. There has been in this state from the start a conflict that never should have existed but I suppose it was inevitable. First of all, and it still exists and is still a reality, a rivalry between Lexington and Louisville. When Lexington existed as the main western frontier town, it was a proud town. Then came the advent in 1811--reaching a point of practical use by 1817 and 1818--of the steamboat. Then, inevitably, the area about the Falls of the Ohio would become the major trading and commercial center of Kentucky. There is no mystery about the growth of Louisville. There has been sort of an insidious rivalry between Louisville and Lexington ever since 1820.

B. C.: Some people perceive a social and political separation between Louisville and the rest of the state as well.

T. C.: I was leading up to that. That is a little bit difficult to explain and I am not sure that I am competent to explain why that is, but I am going to suggest some things that are indicative of that.

First, Louisville became the major urban center in a state that was intensely rural, and where the world whirled around courthouses in small, dusty provincial country towns. That was a world which had no real capability or capacity for understanding the ways of more sophisticated urban life, or industrial and commercial life. Louisville became a manufacturing and distribution center, and railway, newspaper, and educational center and of more sophisticated forms of culture. It became the "state's city". In the make-up of the Louisville population there was a heavy influx of German and Irish immigrants in the 1840's. Then there came that conflict, the "Bloody Monday", which was socially and politically unsettling.

B. C.: What was "Bloody Monday"?

T. C.: That was just a downright civil outbreak, a headbreaking, murderous conflict in 1855 that involved the central area of Louisville, down along the river front and almost as far up as Broadway. It was a fight between Catholics and Protestants, between the German and Anglo elements of the population. It had various sources--principally religious, sociological, nationalistic cultures.

Another fact developed in Louisville that surely has some bearing, I think... maybe I'll say two facts.

Number one, Louisville developed as a rail center with the main line of the Louisville and Nashville Railroad connecting north and south. There developed that bitter rivalry to prevent the central Kentucky area and Cincinnati from developing a competitive system of railroads connecting the South. Finally, in the 1880's, the Cincinnati-Southern Railroad was chartered, but not until a very unseemly fight had developed and you had polarized in the legislature the friction and the conflict between Bluegrass Kentucky and the Ohio falls areas. Out of that came the wielding of powerful political influence on the part of the L & N Railroad, which prevailed right down into the first quarter of this century. Only in the last 40 or 50 years has the grip of the L & N, politically, on this state been relaxed.

Louisville developed a "machine politics" or a "Ward-

Heel" type local politics and the rest of the state has been dubious of that kind of action. There have been, however, rural courthouse rings, heaven knows, there have been 120 county courthouse rings--there still are. The courthouse has been the "eye" of the political storm in Kentucky. Rural Kentucky is not used to the urban type of political management. That has been a factor. I suppose if you come down to simplistic terms, the old rural suspicion of the city has been imagined and magnified all out of proportion. But nevertheless, I think it's been a reality. This state has cut its nose off to spite its political face in this area.

Louisville has produced some very able political talent. There could have come from Louisville some very good governors. A candidate for governor from Louisville had almost no chance of being elected. Lawrence Wetherby was accused of being from Louisville, and he had a difficult time establishing the fact that he was from LaGrange, and not from Louisville. To get tarred with the Louisville brush in the past has not been a political asset.

B. C.: Do you have any idea, off the top of your head, how many governors we've had from Louisville?

T. C.: We've had none that I know of. I can't think of a single one.

B. C.: What about Willson?

T. C.: Maybe Augustus Willson, I believe he did come from Louisville. Beckham had some later Louisville associations I believe. But I would have to check on that. I do not recall any other governor who came from Louisville.

B. C.: With all this fragmentation and contrast, is there such a thing as a typical Kentuckian?

T. C.: I would not think so, no. I feel fairly safe in giving this positive-negative answer. Is there a typical American? Is there a typical anybody? Or a typical Tennessean or Ohioan? I taught at Kent State University and I made the startling discovery that there is a wide gulf between southern and northern Ohio. I cannot be too certain about this, but I do not believe that there is any state in the Union where there is a typical inhabitant. I think we are dealing with a frivolous subject when state people boast that they are typical something. The American geography is too diversified to produce in a common mold a personality that would characterize a region or a state. There is no such thing as a "southerner". Those of us born in the lower South look with some degree of suspicion on those in the upper South. Who is a Southerner?

You could hardly say that Joe Dokes out here is a typical Kentuckian because there are differences. There are differences in outlook, in economic background, all sorts of differences. That gives variety to the state. It would be pretty boring if we were all alike, or if there was a single homogenized Kentucky personality. We boast about a lot of things. Kentucky, I think, should stop and reassess its images. This matter of everybody being crazy about horses--thousands of Kentuckians do not know anything about horses. This matter of everybody being crazy about liquor, and you have got the majority of the counties that vote dry. And the matter of the "Colonel", the goateed colonel--you almost wonder how that got into the imagery of Kentucky. You run around drinking mint juleps out of plastic cups on Derby Day and being somehow or other in the minds of somebody, characteristic of Kentucky. Then there's the idea that we spend the other twelve months of the year drinking juleps. Well, it would be difficult to find a barkeeper in Kentucky who could make an old-fashioned Kentucky julep, or who even knows the recipe for making one. The whiskey image, the tobacco image, and the fair women--of course, there are beautiful women in Kentucky, nobody's going to argue with that. Kentucky doesn't have a monopoly on these things. Sometimes I think we boast about these superficial things in order to cover up the realities that beset this state. I think it is a form of sociological whistling in the dark in the face of so many realistic challenges. Too, it is commercially profitable on occasions.

B. C.: What are those challenges and what are our weaknesses?

T. C.: I am not a prophet. Things can take sudden new directions, there can arise forces which completely reverse trends. But if you read all the things that are being said right now and you pay attention to the straws in the wind, Kentucky stands at this moment, almost as it never has stood before, in a revolutionary moment in its history.

By that I mean the industrial structure is changing. The coal industry in western Kentucky has faded badly from what it was. That does not mean that the coal industry has disappeared, but it is not the major industry that it was. The Kentucky family farm has become highly capitalized and commercialized, more and more edging into the area of agri-business farming rather than subsistence farming. There is coming a fundamental change in the urban structure in the state. Louisville has lost a lot of industries. It has suffered some heavy blows and is getting ready to suffer another one that I hope will not be too severe in the sale of the *Courier-Journal*.

The basic area in which Kentucky is facing a revolution is the employability of its people. That is, not enough of its people are skilled and educated to the point of being adaptable enough that they can retrain as industrial changes occur. The prophets are saying that every five years a lot of these industries are going to have to retrain their labor forces to serve an evolving industry. This all boils down to one big word--education. Never, never has education had so much meaning in the lives of Kentuckians as right now. You wonder if this fact is sufficiently developed in the minds of Kentuckians to really meet the challenges of the twenty-first century

We have come out of a legislative session in which, I think, by and large the legislature and the governor's administration have done better by education than any other past administration's legislative session. This could also be a serious handicap in that the people might jump to the conclusion that they have solved something. They have not. They have only started on the road to meeting the challenges that lie out in the future. If Kentuckians are to be competitive in a technological and industrial society, which so-called informed seers say is coming this way, then they have got to be educated. They have got to be developed into adaptable human beings who can be retrained periodically. Otherwise, you are going to have a large portion of your population almost wholly dependent on public welfare. The main thing I am saying here is that education may have been, I don't think so, but it may have been, in the past, a luxury. It may have been a thing that a large segment of the population could do without and make a living. But that day is over. That day definitely has ended.

I am talking like a prophet, but I think there are already enough signs and documentary data available that a historian is not venturing too far out on a limb to say that changes have already occurred, and the process is ongoing. You see the process in action in so many areas, and this will become progressively more in evidence.

This sounds like a Chamber of Commerce statement about Kentucky. Kentucky can do anything that it sets its mind to do, within reason. It has limitations, every state in the Union has limitations, and Kentucky is no exception. Kentucky never has used to the fullest extent its potentialities as a progressive state. It is going to have to make some radical changes, and those changes are going to hurt. They are going to be costly.

It has to change its outmoded constitution. If it does not rewrite and bring into its modern functioning political society a constitution that permits a state government to operate effectively and efficiently, then Kentucky is going to be handicapped. It has been, and it has suffered tremendously from this constitutional handicapping. As I see it, it cannot go on in the future circumventing and muddling through its constitutional problems. Kentuckians historically have not voted for constitutional changes. They have a fear that is groundless. They are afraid that if they vote to change the constitution some radical group will gain control of the convention and will draw up a radical document and get it adopted and turn Kentucky into a chaotic state. I feel they must think it will turn into one of the Russian satellite states, to hear the opponents of revision talk. There is not a chance in the world of that happening. The chances are on the other side that they will not be liberal enough, that they will not be substantial enough to see that we fundamentally and philosophically release the full energy of the state--the full economic, political, and intellectual energies so the state can progress into a new economic and socially changing age with as few outmoded restrictions as possible.

B. C.: Do you think a new Constitution should be the top priority as far as our future is concerned?

T. C.: I have never wavered on that. I, of course, express a personal opinion, but it is also backed up by a considerable amount of documentation. So much time and energy in this state has been expended getting around the old constitution. That is one thing which goes far to account for Kentucky's backwardness.

You may say, "Why do Mississippi and Kentucky and Arkansas, states like that, stand at the bottom of the comparative statistical tables?" They are all old agricultural states which have not, until recent years, become heavily industrialized. They have not been attractive to more desirable types of industries, partly because of uneducated personnel, of living conditions, or community development not being attractive to the location of a more sophisticated industry. All sorts of things figured in this. That is true here in Kentucky. Many of Kentucky's communities are not attractive enough to the location of industry to bring managerial personnel and settle them down in places which have inadequate medical, library, educational, public health, law enforcement, or efficient local governmental facilities. You can go right down the list.

However, I think there is a very positive fact that must be re-emphasized. We are in a state of revolution and we are going to see the full impact of it coming quicker than you might think. I think there is more awareness in the Kentucky mind of this than has ever been true in the history of the state. I think there is more sensitivity to the need to make change and the willingness to make changes. A thing that we have only seen the tip of is the coming of the Toyota business. I hear on the radio and television and read in the newspapers about the social and political planning that is going on in the Scott County area that has got to take place. You are in an area where a tremendous amount of planning needs to be done for the whole state.

We are not going to erase 120 counties from Kentucky's excessive number. It would be nonsense for me to sit here and say that we are going to do that. I think it would be one of the most progressive things that could happen in Kentucky if you could just wipe off the board 120 political entities called counties. You can even call them districts or call them anything you want to. You can retain the names from now until kingdom come, but you are gradually going to have to revise and consolidate a lot of things that have been the responsibilities of the counties in the past by a force of necessity. For instance, just the simple matter of jails. Kentucky has developed so many criminal problems that now district jails would be much more efficient than local ones. Or district hospitals would be of much more service than every community trying to maintain a hospital. In the educational system, if we erased the old district lines, the old county lines, and followed more rational districting of the educational institutionalizing process, we would be much better off. It is nonsense to maintain 120 county courthouses with 120 official facilities in this time of modern travel and communications. I think the old circuit court system said something along that score. You have several counties represented by a judicial district with the agencies of the court functioning in a district rather than within a confined county limitation. I have never heard any reaction against this. There may be a lot of times when persons have not been very happy about jury selection or having a prosecutor come in from outside of the county, or a judge come in from the outside. In so many areas, the traditional English county system of local government has become outmoded. This has caused the state to assume many county functions.

B. C.: Let's go to A.O. Stanley, because you told me an interesting story one time about your meeting him in Washington. Would A.O. Stanley be, in your estimation, the most colorful governor Kentucky has ever had?

T. C.: I will say this to take out proper historical insurance. He was certainly one of the most colorful. Immediately, you get into the category of Chandler, for instance. Chandler was a colorful figure, and still is.

But back to Stanley. There are things that I have learned that have disappointed me about Governor Stanley. I read a manuscript book where a certain man in the mountains ran a store and was notorious for getting women customers into the store and trading dresses for such commodities as they had to peddle, and he was pretty successful at that business. He got too friendly with a fellow's wife and he and the wife's husband got into a potential shooting situation. The storekeeper kept a rifle in a hole in the ceiling of his store. When he saw the husband coming, he shot him dead. And there was no mistaking the direction that the bullet came from and the level or its course. The sheriff in that case rooted around and discovered this loose plank behind which the newly fired rifle was hidden. It still had the fresh smell of powder and the empty shell in the chamber. The storekeeper was convicted of murder and sent to the penitentiary for life. He sent an agent to Frankfort with a briefcase packed neatly with $100,000 in new bills. And when this prisoner arrived to report to the warden of the penitentiary, there was a nice pardon all sealed and delivered, and A. O. Stanley received a nice present of $100,000. The murderer had a pardon.

B. C.: What were your impressions of Stanley when you met him?

T. C.: Oh, he was a marvelous old man. He was a superb story teller. Bill Townsend had managed his campaign in the Bluegrass and he used to tell me so many stories about Stanley. He had become a legend with me before I ever saw him. I do not know exactly how I got acquainted with him.

He would come into Lexington and I would go to see him, or he would tell me he was coming and I would be on the lookout for him. He loved to tell stories. He would tell those stories about Edwin Morrow and that campaign and poking fun at Ed, but loving him every step of the way.

Stanley just missed having his name established in American history in the labor field. He had originated what became the eight-hour law, the Clayton Act. He was actually the author of the Clayton Act, but Clayton by some kind of Senate maneuver got his name attached to it instead of Stanley. Stanley just missed immortality.

Then he served on the International Boundary Commission. He used to sit and talk to me about being on that Commission. That, to him, appealed to his sense of humor. He had a Canadian counterpart. They would get an ample supply of liquor and after they had gotten themselves well oiled for two or three days, they'd go out and look at the boundary and say, "We agree--it's still there." Then, they would come home and report on the boundary. There's no telling what the problems were with the boundary, but they did not find any.

You know, Eisenhower tried to fire him. But in the round, the President fired the wrong Stanley. He fired a good loyal Republican instead. Well, the old man got quite a humorous kick out of that.

He used to tell me the story about violating the "Hatch Act." I think Keen Johnson was running for governor, and he had Stanley make a speech for him. Stanley couldn't legally make a political speech under the Hatch Act. At that time he was on the Federal Boundary Commission. He stopped in Morehead and a crowd had come to see the old man and hear his famous oratory. Stanley said, "You know, I'd just give anything to have this Hatch Act out of the way. If we didn't have the Hatch Act, here's what I'd say, but I can't say it because of the Hatch Act, but here's what I would say." Then he'd go ahead and deliver one rip-snorting speech. But he said, "I can't say that to you because of the Hatch Act." Well, he was a smooth old cooter. And just by knowing him, I was very much attracted to him.

When my children were young--my son Bennett and my

daughter Elizabeth--we wanted them to see something of the national capital, and take them around to various places. I wrote Tom Underwood that we were coming. Tom was then in the Senate. I wanted him to get me tickets to get into the Senate gallery and around. When we got to Washington, we went to Tom's office and met him coming through the door just like a wild bull. He said, "They're having a hearing on tobacco and I've got to go down there, but I'm behind time." And he said, "Go on in and Christine will take care of you." Christine was Keen Johnson's sister. We went inside to sit down and talk to Christine. She got out some cards and some tickets.

We started walking around the Senate Office Building halls and came upon Margaret Chase Smith's office. We knew her and saw her name on the door and stopped to look at it and she came up and said, "Come on in and let's have a visit."

So, we went in and she said, "I've got to change my dress." She went behind a little screen and changed her dress, talking to us all the time. We sat and talked to Mrs. Smith until it was time to get some lunch. We had not had a chance to use our tickets. So, we went on around and joined Tom Underwood and Earl Clements. We had not had a chance to go to Clements' office. I was embarrassed because there was Earl and I hadn't been to his office. It did not seem to make any difference with him. Then Tom said, "We are going to have an exciting luncheon today." Just at that time I looked down the hall and saw what he was talking about. There came the old Senator of boundary line fame.

B. C.: A. O. Stanley.

T. C.: Yes. He said he was going to have lunch with us. We got into the Senate dining room and seated with two children, one on each side of Senator Stanley. You cannot imagine a much more unusual situation than that--two kids sitting beside old Stanley, and Stanley telling his stories.

He didn't care what he said. He got to telling a story about going to see his cousin Margaret. He said, "Cousin

Margaret met me at the train with a jug of wine. She said, 'Cousin Owsley, you've just got to help me. These brothers of mine are trying to take part of Pa's estate away from me. You've just got to help me.' " So, he went up and stayed two days, drinking that wine and I don't know what else he was drinking.

And he told me, "I had to get back to Washington. So I got on a train and went back to Washington, and was gone about two or three days and I came back to Richmond and Cousin Margaret met me at the train and said, 'Oh, Cousin Owsley, we're in terrible trouble here. The gossips are now saying that you and I were up there dead drunk for two days and they're telling it all over Richmond.' " Stanley said, "How long did they say that was?" And she said, "Two days." He said, "Two days? Hell, that's a lie. I've been drunk all my life!"

With him it was just one story like that after another.

He came here to Lexington--he had an old friend, Roy Williams, the postmaster. Roy knew the old man upside down, and he would serve him bourbon in a tea glass, one tea-glass full of bourbon after another. But on this occasion, Stanley was going to speak to the Kiwanis Club. Roy got a little overgenerous with his bourbon.

It would happen that on that day there was a Baptist convention of some sort, and about two-thirds of the audience was made up of Baptist preachers. There Stanley was, tighter than a barrel hoop, and he got up telling about Tom Marshall in Buffalo. I don't know how he got on to this story, but he was telling how Marshall was speaking somewhere and somebody back in the crowd said, "Louder!" Marshall finally raised his voice just as loud as he could speak, and the fellow was still yelling, "Louder!" The story was that Marshall stopped and said, "When Gabriel blows his horn, there will be some fool in Buffalo yelling 'Louder, Gabriel, louder!' " Except Stanley, with all those Baptist preachers sitting out in front, said, "When Gabriel blows his horn, there will be some Goddamn fool sitting out there yelling 'Louder, Gabriel, louder!' " I wish you could have seen the expression on those Baptist preachers' faces.

Well, Ed Morrow and Stanley had been opponents in a

hot gubernatorial campaign over no real important issue. Morrow, a Republican, advocated taking the dog tax off. Stanley did not advocate anything except getting Stanley elected governor. Stanley told me he was speaking to the Democrats downstairs in the Madison County courthouse in Richmond and Morrow was speaking to the Republicans upstairs. Stanley stopped in the middle of his speech and howled like a dog at the Republicans. Now this was around 1916, and in the days when candidates rode mules to remote places and these fellows travelled around together. They would speak in courthouses and just give each other unshirted hell, then they would get on their mules and ride to the next place, sleep together, drink together, and get up the next day and tear the shirt off of each other, and all about the meaningless dog tax.

Anyway, Stanley said he was speaking to the Democrats downstairs in the Madison County Courthouse and he didn't have anything much to say to them. He knew he already had them. He could hear the Republicans upstairs, and he just stopped in the middle of his speech and put his hand up to his mouth and howled like a dog to stir up the animals upstairs.

I remember another amusing Stanley story. During a hotly contested campaign for governor, they met each other on a street in Bardstown one day. He saw Morrow coming and Morrow saw him at the same time. Morrow walked over to the other side of the street and came right by him, looked at him but never spoke to him. So Stanley turned around and said, "Ed, what's the matter with you? Do you mean you're going by here and not speaking to me? Are you mad at me?" And then Morrow said, "I am mad at you. I am fighting mad at you." And Stanley said, "Why are you mad at me?" Morrow said, "All these years you've run up and down this state telling lies on me. You've told a thousand lies on me. But now you're running up and down the state telling the truth and that hurts."

They remained bosom friends. Mrs. Stanley told me that the Morrows would come over to their apartment in Washington and have dinner and Stanley and Morrow would get off and drink together and spin their yarns. They would have a hard time getting them to the dinner table.

B. C.: Have you ever reflected upon who were the greatest governors of this state?

T. C.: Yes, I have. Before I talk about great governors and picking out--like some omnipotent person I am not--I would like to say this. In picking out certain individuals and labeling them "great", you may be doing other people unforgivable injury. Every man serves his time in his times, and the times are never the same--the issues are never the same, neither are the demands and challenges. You have to keep these facts in mind.

I would say that you would have to put Isaac Shelby in a selective category. He was not a great statesman. He was not a great thinker. He was not a great administrator as far as I know. He was on the scene. He was a leader. There is not any doubt about that. His record confirms that. He was on the scene at the right time and the right place. He assumed the leadership of the organization of the state in 1792. You could hardly say that the first Shelby administration did more than organize this state and get state government to functioning. The second time around, he proved a great leader in the War of 1812. He was a right impressive influence in that period of the war. Actually getting the legislature's permission for him to leave the state to head a military force--you know there is a provision in the Kentucky Constitution that forbids the governor to lead a militia force--they gave Shelby an exceptional privilege of authority. I think I can say without much fear of being contradicted that Shelby would have to be considered a highly competent governor in his time and under prevailing circumstances.

You drift along from one governor to another--who in that crowd was a stand out? The book edited by Lowell Harrison that has just come out, *Kentucky Governors*, is a very interesting book, and a very useful one. The people who wrote the various biographical sketches made some evaluation of the governors.

A governor that had the potential of being a really good

governor and leading this state in the right direction in a seminal moment is a little-known name among them--Gabriel Slaughter. I do not know if anyone would pick him as a great governor or not. He was in such conflict with the legislature. He had a lot of good ideas but he was never able to put them to use.

B. C.: When was he governor?

T. C.: From 1818 or 1819--in that period, or 1820-21.

You can come on down and I think John J. Crittenden made a good governor. I have never seen anything to the contrary. He was certainly capable of making a good governor.

We have dragged out three in that early period. We come to the post Civil War period and the two men who stand out--one who had the greatest potential was Luke P. Blackburn. He had some clay in his feet--that of releasing convicts because of bad prison conditions and his overgenerosity of pardoning the less criminally charged prisoners from the penitentiary. He had the potential of being a great governor. I do not think there would be any argument over Simon Buckner. If I were to pick only one out of the post Civil War period it would be Buckner, as being the most solid of the immediate post Civil War governors.

B. C.: Do you have any particular reason?

T. C.: Yes. Many reasons. First of all, he had a very high capability as a leader in military training and he was a good businessman. He was a wealthy man. He did not have to steal anything. He was governor of this state when the state desperately needed that kind of leadership. Now, when it comes to saying that he exercised a lot of vision, I think maybe there would be some argument. In education, for instance. This state was terribly poor--just dog poor and it was hard for a governor to do much more than day-to-day operations. It was hard for him to project any kind of program. And he always had that millstone around his neck with the legislature. There were good legislators and there were poor and venal ones. As it happened, Kentucky, like the other states, had a lot of defective legislators.

In this century, I think you would find people who would say that within the context of the times and conditions, J. C. W. Beckham made a reasonably good governor. I think some people say that Augustus E. Willson made a reasonably good governor. Look at the problems that man faced.

If Happy Chandler had served out any four year term as governor, with the latter two years being as successful as his first two of each term, he would have been one of the standout governors of Kentucky. He helped to reorganize the state and bring its government officially out of the nineteenth century. One thing, in my personal opinion, that weakened Happy's claim was the repeal of the sales tax at a time when the state so desperately needed that financial source. Later it was returned. It had to be reintroduced. Under the Combs administration and under the Nunn administration, they had to turn to the sales tax to meet educational and veteran bonus demands.

If I had to live day to day with Earle Clements, I would have found it pretty trying, because Earle was high-tempered and demanding. Nevertheless, notwithstanding, Earle Clements made a forceful governor. There were a lot of things that he did. He got Section 246 out of the Constitution. If that $5,000 salary limitation had remained, it would have bankrupted the state.

B. C.: That was a $5,000 limitation on spending?

T. C.: On salaries and pensions. Then the court handed down its famous "Rubber-Dollar" decision. It takes some explaining to describe what the "Rubber-Dollar" decision was. It was simply the riding on an economic index on what the dollar was worth in 1950 as compared with its worth in 1890 in regards to purchasing power.

I do not think Earle was strong with the rural road program, the breaking down of barriers and isolation and I think he was reasonably honest. I do not think he was guilty of any major graft. I suppose the most money that Earle got was money contributed to campaign "kitties". He, however, was not the only one who ever received that benefit and will not be the last.

I do not think there is any doubt about Lawrence Wetherby. Lawrence was not a sensational governor. He was not a flamboyant or boasting governor. As a matter of fact, a lot of people looked on him as a weak governor in many ways. But when you think about some of the things that Lawrence did--one of them was building that turnpike from Louisville to Elizabethtown. Would not this state have been in a mess with that choker on its main north-south highways? Happy Chandler campaigned against that saying it started nowhere and went nowhere, when you got on it you couldn't get off and when you got off you couldn't get on. That was all nonsense. Now they have just reworked that road. I think it is six lanes. It is a major linkage in the north-south I-65.

Where Lawrence really stood up and got himself counted was as presiding officer of the Southern Governor's Conference. He kept things reasonably quiet there in that early phase after the U. S. Supreme Court *Brown vs. School Board* decision. When the court rendered its decision, Wetherby said, "Kentucky would have to do what it took to obey the law." In my opinion, Wetherby was a constructive governor in a time which demanded courage and gumption.

B. C.: In what way did he keep things quiet? What do you mean?

T. C.: They didn't pass any rash resolutions and go dashing onto the battlefield of desegregation, as some southern states did later in the Citizen's Council business--the Southern Manifesto initiated by Jim Eastland, Senator Byrd and others. Wetherby fended that sort of thing off. Here in Kentucky, when the newspaper boys rushed to his office on May 17, 1954, and asked him what he was going to do in response to the Brown desegregation decision, he made the wisest statement of any southern governor. He said, "We're going to do what it takes to obey the law." And he very calmly went about doing that. He saved Kentucky an awful lot of emotional and legal wear and tear. Later, under the Chandler administration, we had the Sturgis and Clays situation. Then even later-- I have forgotten who was governor, but Judge Jim Gordon was on the Federal Court-- all that commotion came up in Louisville about busing. Otherwise, Kentucky was reasonably quiet and has remained quiet to its eternal credit. Resisting civil rights could have hurt this state terribly.

I do not think there is any doubt but that Bert Combs made a good governor. Bert did not make a saintly or a perfect governor. He would be the first to say that. In the field of education, he gave his full and effective support. He opened the way for modern educational expansion. Among his many accomplishments, he greatly extended the toll turnpike system.

B. C.: Ruby Laffoon--you didn't mention.

T. C.: No, I do not consider him one of the great governors either. I think he was conscientious, and the old man did the best he could in hard depression years.

B. C.: He placed the three cent sales tax during the depression.

T. C.: He undertook to meet the needs of the state, and especially those of an improved school system.

B. C.: And Lieutenant Governor Chandler had it repealed by special call of the legislature when Governor Laffoon was out of the state, and that created a tremendous uproar.

T. C.: And then Tom Rhea and Ruby Laffoon held out for that double primary which got them defeated.

B. C.: That was one of the great ironies of Kentucky history-- Happy Chandler becoming governor because of a change in the election law which he opposed.

T. C.: That's right. In answering the question about governors of Kentucky and their possible rankings, one would have to conclude there is limited historical value in such an evaluation. No two governors of Kentucky served under precisely the same conditions of the times and state of affairs in the Commonwealth. Although all of them were mandated by the constitution of the state to bear certain responsibilities, their four-year administrations faced different challenges. A safer evaluation would be one which dealt with how well individual governors met their specific challenges. In the first three-quarters of a century there was a sharp contrast between the problems confronted by Isaac Shelby during his two administrations and those which confronted Beriah Magoffin in the era of the outbreak of the Civil War. In the middle period, 1865-1915, there arose new and different challenges. For instance, the modernization of education, dealing with transportation, the eastern mountain feuds, the Black Patch War, and state finances. Certainly in this era Governor Simon Bolivar Buckner must be considered a better than average governor.

Governors after 1915 faced the problems of two world wars, of labor unrest in the mining sections, the Great Depression, creating a modern highway system, improving schools, and matters of public health. A criteria which might be applied to every gubernatorial administration would be how much did the incumbent do to improve conditions in the Commonwealth. There were "turn-around" governors who fostered far-reaching legislation. Governor Chandler recognized an imperative need for drastically reorganizing the processes of administrative government. The Reorganization Act of 1937 dragged the Commonwealth out of the nineteenth century into the twentieth. One reads this act and the history of its application and wonders how the state operated under the archaic system of the nineteenth century. Governor Chandler could count this as one of his most important accomplishments.

Governor Earle Clements could make claim of three or four significant redirections of Kentucky government. He was able to secure the revision of section 246 of the

Constitution limiting salaries of state officials. Had this not been done the state would have suffered irretrievable damage. Clements contributed materially to educational advancements, and the farm-to-market legislation establishing a rural highway system went far toward breaking the isolative barriers which have divided the Commonwealth in almost every public area.

Governor Lawrence Wetherby must be credited with major accomplishments in keeping the Commonwealth relatively calm in the face of the great emotional period of applying the court mandates in *Brown vs. Topeka School Board.* Too, his support of the superhighway system in the construction of the Elizabethtown-Louisville Toll Road was a long step into modernity.

The Bert Combs administration was a major landmark in turning the state around in support of public education, the construction of highways, the parks system, public health, and beautification plus many other advances.

Governor Edward Breathitt furthered the breaking of isolation in Kentucky by building more toll roads, a move which is now paying off in the freeing of these highways from toll. He undertook to revise the archaic constitution by holding a convention to draft a model constitution. Had the people accepted this constitution, the state would be well on its way to solving some of its most pressing problems. Certainly the governmental reorganization under the Ford administration is a landmark in Kentucky history. Governor Louis Nunn presided over the state in one of its most feverish social moments.

Thus, each governor's administration has to be measured, not against those of his or her predecessors, but against the issues of the moment and how well they dealt with them. Some governors have demonstrated far more courage and imagination than others, but all of them more or less have reflected in their administrations the temper of the people themselves.

B. C.: In Kentucky, the governor cannot act as governor when they are out of the state. Is that unique to Kentucky?

T. C.: No, I think you would find that in other states. The lieutenant governor in most, if not all states, acts in the absence of the governor.

B. C.: Is that constitutional provision archaic, in your opinion?

T. C.: No, not really. There is great danger in permitting the governor to act as governor from outside the state. He could form a coup of some sort and go outside and do heinous things, and be beyond the constabulary reach of the state to arrest him. I can think of several reasons why it would not be wise to let him exercise gubernatorial powers outside the state. If a lieutenant governor does something wrong as acting governor, he would have to get in a car or grab a plane quickly to get to the state border before the state police could catch him. That is, if they knew about it at the time. If the governor was allowed to act outside the state, he might possibly transfer large amounts of money and be beyond the reach of Kentucky law.

B. C.: So you think this particular provision is not outdated but should be maintained?

T. C.: Surely, you might have another thing. You might have a governor say, "I believe I will spend the next three months in Florida, and I am just going down and hole up." Well, things could go to rack and ruin back at home and that official's off out of the state. There are all sorts of reasons why that restriction should be kept.

B. C.: *Why has there been so much violence in Kentucky and in the South?*

T. C.: This is an extremely complex sociological, economic and political issue. There are all sorts of strands that go into the historical tapestry of the history of violence.

Kentucky was a frontier state. From the time the first Anglo-American settlers crossed the eastern mountain range and came down the Ohio River to the area that is now the Commonwealth of Kentucky, there was violence involved. Over and over and over in the documenting of the frontier experience, there are stories of Indian skirmishes, Indian battles, raids, or personal confrontations. The story of Daniel Boone, for instance, and his family is one of coming sometimes to violent ends, especially in the death of his son in that raid on Cumberland Gap.

When the frontier period was over, then Kentucky became involved in other things. It came pretty close to an open conflict with the Spanish government when it refused to surrender Louisiana after the Louisiana Purchase. Kentuckians were actually armed, ready to go to war over that issue, if necessary. That issue was settled sensibly.

Then came the river. I am not sure how much impact the river had on the Kentucky population, generally, but the story of rivermen, flatboatmen, and later on, steamboatmen, all had to do with a certain amount of personal conflict and personal violence. The War of 1812 was a bloody affair as far as Kentucky was concerned. The Battle of Tippecanoe, for instance, resulted in disaster for Kentuckians, in which a very prominent man, Joseph Hamilton Daviess, was killed.

Then you had the Battle of the Thames, Frenchtown, the Battle of the Raisin, and others. All of those things contributed to the developing of violent situations, as did the Battle of New Orleans. For years after the Battle of New Orleans, there was an argument that went on between John Adair and Andrew Jackson over the role of Kentuckians, especially on the west bank of that conflict.

Then there came up the period, from about 1820 down to 1850, in which duelling became a practice. I doubt that I would be historically correct in saying it was a common practice. Nevertheless, it was a practice in Kentucky history. It was during that time when the oath was written in the Kentucky Constitution which asked elected public officials to swear that they had not fought a duel or carried a challenge or served as a second in a duel.

Then the Mexican War was contributory. A great many Kentuckians went away to the Mexican War and experienced a certain amount of violence, as any war was bound to generate, and that one did generate a considerable amount.

Of course, the big chapter, the period of the Civil War. The Civil War history was more notable, not for the major battles that were fought in Kentucky, but for the raids, the skirmishes and for the third-party war--the activities of the guerillas. Those things touched off a tremendous amount of violence. One factor, the organization of the home guards to protect Kentucky's neutrality, with the Confederate Army on one side and the Union Army on the other, was bound to result in a certain amount of conflict.

Following the war, you had two or three major chapters. First, the outbreak of the feuds in the eastern Appalachian area. On one occasion I went through the records of Pike County during the Civil War and into the reconstruction period. I discovered in those records how intense the feeling was toward the guerillas and the raiders. I am certainly not making any pretense of being especially informed on the feuds. I am sure that in those records was a strong thread of evidence that the Hatfield-McCoy feud had about as much in its background arising out of the irregularities, conflicts, and animosities developed in the war as the conflict over the so-called pig and the intermarriage of those families.

Then, in the turn of the nineteenth century into the twentieth century, you had that very strong political conflict that arose in which the farmers, the agrarians, sometimes called the progressives, were in conflict with the very conservative--or brigadier--power structure and the exploitive activities of the L & N Railroad.

In the election of 1899 and 1900, in which William Goebel was a Democratic nominee and William S. Taylor was the Republican nominee, you had a bitter hard-fought campaign. The result of that was a disputed election over the issue of tissue paper ballots and other election irregularities. The climax was the assassination of William Goebel. No incident in Kentucky history has ever had the acute, unsettling and long-lingering impact as that incident had. It took Kentucky at least three decades to get over the conflict of the Goebel affair. That touched off all sorts of violent reactions. As a matter of fact, there was a strong element of eastern Kentucky feuding groups that got mixed up in the mountain army which went to Frankfort. For instance, the Hargis-Cockerel feud in Breathitt County, or the Baker-White-Garrard-Howard feud in Manchester, Clay County, and other groups of the mountain army that came from all over eastern Kentucky was simply an expression of violent intent and in some cases violent outbreaks.

In the agricultural field, all of the unrest, all of the exploitations, all of the animosities generated by the market and pricing practices by the corporations causing the Black Patch War, which was an act of violence. The Night Rider activities was an expression of violence. The real battles contributed to a certain element of violence.

Kentucky is still a violent state. You hardly pick up the morning paper without reading of some murder or the commitment of some crime in the state that is simply unbelievable--almost beyond belief as a human act. An element of Kentucky's population appears to be little better than beasts.

Violence is a very good field and a very useful field for the writing of a book. It's not going to be a pretty book; it's not going to praise Kentuckians; it's not going to improve the image of this state. But nevertheless, it will bring this matter out in the open so that an intelligent reading public can develop a comprehensive understanding and may set some intelligent actions to alleviate this shameful outbreak of violence that occurs year in and year out. Professor Robert Ireland of the University of Kentucky Department of History has underway a study of violence. He is a reputable historian and has published two books of first rate quality on Kentucky history. I predict that this will be an eye-opening volume. Again, I think it will not be a pretty story. It will not be a pleasing story. It will not be one of "moonlight and roses". But it will be a cold, harsh statement of realities that must be reckoned with.

B. C.: Kentucky is a conservative state in many respects, and is part of the Bible Belt. Yet it has strong economic ties to whiskey, horse racing, and tobacco, which, of course, are perceived by fundamentalists, at least, to be the great evils of life. How do you account for that paradox?

T. C.: Well, let us take whiskey first. This state was settled by an Anglo-American population--English and Scotch, Irish and Welsh, in about that descending order. Three of these national groups had strong tastes and traditions of whiskey in their backgrounds. Scotch almost means whiskey. The Irish and the Welsh maybe a little less so, but just by a degree, and the English less so. I do not think the English were as fond of whiskey as were the other groups. Then, of course, there was the German element that settled here with the liquor, whiskey and beer tradition.

The farmers who came in here and began farming this frontier land produced large quantities of grain and fruits. They had no way to sell that produce on the local market. They could not barter it because everybody else had a supply of grain. The one way they could transport it without spoilage was to convert it into distilled spirits. That went for both fruit and grain. Right on down to the present moment, whiskey became a very important fact in Kentucky's economic life. You had domestic distillers--farmers who might have been the staunchest church members you could imagine--converting their grain crops into an exportable, manageable, preservable commodity. The tradition of making whiskey in Kentucky is strong. Second, it was big money. Another thing is that there was a rationalization on the part of a lot of people. It does not seem reasonable--it isn't reasonable--that a state that has been so firmly associated with the making of bourbon whiskey and, until recent years, the brewing of beer, should have so many dry counties voted in by the concert of bootleggers and crusading ministers.

Of course, they haven't "dried up" the counties. There is not a truly dry county in this state. Anybody that believes that you have a "dry county" is a very unrealistic individual. I know a county that is "dry" legally, but it could not be much "wetter". The only thing that could dampen it more would be for its liquor sellers to put up signs. I sold a couple a half an acre of land, which I wish to goodness I had never done, thinking they were going to put a trailer on it, at least that is what they told me they were going to do. I expected that they were going to live a quiet family life and look after my front gate to another piece of property. They moved in, they tore the gate down to begin with, and then I began to notice a stream of traffic--an unusual amount--going in. Pretty soon the gossip got to me that they were selling liquor. That is going on in all the "dry" counties. All you have to do if you doubt that is park your car and walk one mile down a roadway in a "dry" county and count the beer cans and liquor bottles that you see along the way. You'll even see aluminum can hunters picking up cans along the way. Now that's part of the "dry" Kentucky.

B. C.: I think there are approximately 90 out of 120 counties that are "dry".

T. C.: I think that is approximately right.

B. C.: What in your estimation would be the economic effect if those counties went "wet"?

T. C.: They would collect the taxes on the sales of liquor and they would have some control over the sale--they could well exercise control over licensing the dealers. I do not think the effect as far as the individual drinking is concerned would be appreciably different one way or the other. Heavens, you go into a town like Richmond in Madison County--liquor stores are all over the place. You would think the business community is made up almost altogether of liquor stores to look at the signs. Those things are the first water holes that a lot of people from the eastern "dry" counties strike. They buy liquor by the carload and take it home to "dry land". I dare say that very few of the sheriffs and law enforcement officials pay a whole lot of attention to it.

B. C.: Do you think that the local option laws are outmoded?

T. C.: They were outmoded to begin with.

B. C.: And do you perceive them changing in the near future?

T. C.: Not really. Not as long as the bootleggers make as much money as they seem to make. They can put a lot of money into a political campaign and vote a county "dry".

B. C.: Wasn't that one of the primary issues in the campaign between Morrow and Stanley--the ""drys" and the "wets"?

T. C.: It had come up in the past, I guess so. Morrow was wet by his drinking habits. I'd have to check and see how much of a factor that was. It may have been the major factor. Neither man could make much of a case for himself as being "dry".

B. C.: You mentioned previously that one of the watershed events in Kentucky was the upswing of evangelism and revival camp meetings in the early 1800's. On balance, has that evangelical fervor and camp revival mentality had a positive or negative effect upon the progress of Kentucky?

T. C.: That would be pretty hard to answer.

A lot of times it thwarted progress. A lot of times it has been reactionary. It reacted negatively to the things that would have been pretty vital in the progress of a community.

The revivalism that we are talking about was conservative. There are no questions about that. It was emotional, and it was revisionary in some respects. The 1801 revival was part of the origin of the annual camp meeting and the annual religious outpourings which were as much social revivals as religious ones. It had a lot to do with the shaping of the collective minds of Kentucky. It developed a lot of prejudices, and a lot of reactions that were not in the best interests of the state which really did not have a whole lot of bearing on the moral tone of the state.

There is an unexplored subject in Kentucky right now that I think might yield some pretty interesting results. Kentucky has had every brand of Baptists that ever lived. It has had a large element that you bring in under just a common grouping of regular Baptists. That includes primitive Baptists, or all sorts of congregational divisions. Those ministers for the most part have not been educated. As a matter of fact, they have opposed education. They have not been sophisticated people, and they have offered to a large number of Kentuckians a negative form of leadership--a reactionary form--that was opposed to education and opposed to any forms of change which might be branded "modernism". When you get back in the isolated rural communities in this state, there is a lot of this attitude still prevalent, which has been greatly expanded and magnified by the rise in this century of the so-called "holiness" or "evangelical" groups that have come into existence. They have exerted an awful lot of subtle influence in Kentucky.

I have not quite said one thing that I would like to express as clearly as I can. That ministerial leadership has been important in the shaping of the mind and the condition of thinking and the condition of reacting to public matters. Too many ministers preached the doctrine, "I don't have an education; I don't need an education to understand the 'word of God' or to preach the 'word of God'. All I need is a call--an emotional call and experience." The "call" has been acclaimed as various things such as being "born again", being "sanctified", or being "called". This attitude has been anti-intellectual. When you have as large an element in a state as you have here in Kentucky of that kind of group thinking, then surely it has, historically, had an impact. Nobody knows how much. A competent sociologist or historian, or a trained theologian could write a very interesting and constructive book--a very serious book--on the shaping of the Kentucky religious and social mind as it has affected public education--the impact of fundamentalism in this state on education.

It's like getting just the slightest concept that there is an animal out there in the dark, but we do not know fully its size or its significance. Oh, yes, a perceptive scholar could come up with a tremendously interesting study.

B. C.: How much of an impact has the Louisville Courier-Journal had on this state?

T. C.: It is very difficult to measure the impact that a newspaper has on a community. About the surest way to measure it would be for the paper to cease publication, and you pretty soon would see some amount of its manifestations. Kentucky has never had a full state newspaper, and never can, really, because the geographical peculiarities of the state make it difficult to distribute from one end to the other a newspaper that is current in the modern sense of the term. The *Courier-Journal* has been "the" state paper. It has been the state editorial voice and news media; it has been the state advertising media as far as that goes. It has been a voice--a clear one--right or wrong in the field of expressing an editorial opinion on all sorts of things. It has been--since the days of the founding of the *Louisville Journal* under the editorship of George D. Prentice-- a strong editorial voice. It has been a newspaper of not only state importance but of regional importance and it has attracted national attention.

To me personally, and I think to the state and to Kentucky people generally, the Bingham relinquishment is disturbing news, highly disturbing news. Nobody else is likely to come in and take the rich, personal place of the Bingham management of the paper. Maybe that sort of management is outmoded and outdated in modern American capital industrial management and organization. Kentucky had better hope that the new owner of the *Courier-Journal* will have an awareness of the problems of the state and its needs, and will be courageous enough to speak out with a clear editorial voice about Kentucky, because Kentucky itself is in a very sensitive area of change and it needs a clear, loud editorial voice.

B. C.: What kind of job do you think we are doing in Kentucky in regards to the preservation of our historic cities and landmarks?

T. C.: We are doing a much better job than we did formerly. Because of the age and historical diversities, we have a large number of landmarks. With the National Registry, we are getting more and more places above the safety net; I suppose there are some places left that should be brought into the National Registry. There are still homes that should be in there. Robert Penn Warren's home in Guthrie, for instance, should be preserved and marked before he passes on. I am on the Markers Commission and I am going to suggest that we put a marker there, because he is easily Kentucky's most famous literary figure of all times. We ought to mark his place. Jesse Stuart's place is marked, I think.

B. C.: Describe some of the national landmark events which have had a great impact on Kentucky.

T. C.: The Great Depression had a very deep impact on Kentucky. Those were days of economic and social stringency. They were days, and I recall personally, in which the outlook was one of near hopelessness, not only for university professors, but for the rank and file of Kentuckians, no matter what their endeavors were. I served as director of the State Historical Records Survey and came in very close contact with the W.P.A. workers. We employed a lot of them in that survey, and I saw how desperately they needed employment just to hold their body and soul together, and how inadequately prepared they were--as a matter of fact, hopelessly unprepared to perform the simple duties that were required of them in that survey.

I also worked with the Kentucky Writer's Project and I saw there the same thing. A lot of people turned writers who never in the world expected to put one sentence after another on a piece of white paper. The great mass of material collected for the preparation of the *Guide to the Bluegrass State* is really an impressive record of the degree of education, the degree of experience, and, I might add, the hopeless inadequacy of those people. Yet, that employment kept them living, and kept them with a slight glimmer of hope until better days could come around again.

I think some more fundamental things occurred in the Great Depression. There was the building campaign of the P.W.A. that resulted in the improvement of school buildings, post offices, courthouses, university buildings and other public structures. In a sense, to a great degree, the Great Depression brought about a modernization of many of Kentucky's outmoded, delapidated facilities.

World War II was simply a dividing line between the ages. World War II utilized the unemployed, either as workers in some kind of war industry, or as soldiers, enlisted men and women in the military services. Of course, there were phenomenal changes in economic conditions with the inflation, with the activities of war. All those things contributed to a marked change in Kentucky.

After World War II, Kentucky was never the same in many respects. In spite of what I said about the reorganization of state government in the 1930's, World War II dragged Kentucky out of the nineteenth century and magnified for it the challenges of a modern post-war age in which Kentucky lived, not as a provincial, isolated Commonwealth. It had suddenly been thrust onto a world-wide stage in which the problems of the world became problems which somehow or other affected the way of life in Kentucky.

I was not in Kentucky when President John F. Kennedy was assassinated. I was staying in a hotel within two blocks of the White House at the time that occurred. I was working in the Library of Congress doing research when a professor from Winthrop College in South Carolina came down and told me that Kennedy had been assassinated--at least there was a rumor that he had been assassinated. We undertook to find out whether that was just a wild rumor or not, and nobody seemed to know. They closed the Library of Congress and as I walked by the national Capitol they were lowering the flag and Congress was adjourning. The Senators and Congressmen, and then the staffs, were walking out the front of the Capitol, and I walked from the Capitol down to Pennyslvania Avenue, all the way to the old Longefellow Hotel just in back of the White House. I think that was one of the weirdest experiences that I have had or ever will have in my life, as far as that is concerned. That was a street which, under ordinary circumstances would be bustling with activity, but simply was like walking through a tomb. It was a vividly strange experience. Even when you saw people, they were virtually speaking in whispers. There was no honking of horns and none of the noise of a great metropolis. It was as if the nation's life had suddenly gone dead. I think that was true in Kentucky, but I was not here at the time, nor was I here during the riots of the 1960's. I am not really capable of commenting on that.

B. C.: Do you have an opinion as to whether Daniel Boone's remains are actually buried in the grave in Frankfort?

T. C.: Right after they brought his remains back here from Missouri, Dr. Robert Peter had a plaster cast made of the skull--Boone's skull. And in the last year, or 15 months or so, a University of Kentucky professor took a look at the skull. He could not tell positively, but he was under the general impression that it is the skull of a white caucasian.

B. C.: Where is that plaster cast of the skull?

T. C.: It is in the Kentucky State Historical Society.

B. C.: In the Archives Building?

T. C.: No. In the old State Office Building.

B. C.: When was Daniel Boone's body brought back here to be buried?

T. C.: I am not sure about the year--I think September 13, 1845. They brought the remains back and had quite a service right before they reburied him. They had the service up on the hill where they buried him and Rebecca in the Frankfort Cemetery overlooking the Kentucky River.

B. C.: When did he die?

T. C.: Just before sunrise, September 26, 1820.

B. C.: So when they exhumed his body and brought it back here, I guess there was just more or less a skeleton left.

T. C.: That's right.

B. C.: And then they made a plaster cast of the skeleton's head at that time.

T. C.: Just of the head, yes. I always intended to take Charlie Snow down to Frankfort to examine it. Charlie was a highly recognized physical anthropologist who worked in Hawaii after the war for the military--when they brought all the bones of soldiers to be identified. You know that is a highly confidential and secretive operation. Charlie died before I could take him down there to examine the Boone cast.

B. C.: Kentucky was one of the first states to allow 18 year olds to vote. How did that come about? Why did a state that had been so politically conservative take the first step with this issue?

T. C.: The enlistment age was lowered, and the attitude was taken that "if they are old enough to go to war, they are old enough to vote." Politicians found that this might be a desirable element to add to the electorate. They might be more easily manipulated than some of the other voters in an election. Too, some of the other states had lowered the voting age. There was also pressure from this age group.

B. C.: Let's talk about women in Kentucky history. How have women fared in Kentucky historically compared to other states?

T. C.: Oh, I suppose the same. There are some states where the activists have been more numerous and more vociferous than in Kentucky. That is a book that some one of these women activists in Kentucky should write--"Women in Kentucky." That is a good story and the material is there waiting. Of course, it must be remembered that Madeline McDowell Breckinridge and Laura Clay were major figures in the suffragette movement.

Let's begin with the women in the state. There are named women and nameless women who are important. You must be aware of the pioneer woman who came early into Kentucky. I do not think we could have settled so quickly and so satisfactorily a wilderness region without the help of women. They brought three elements into Kentucky that were important. First was an element of social stability. By that I mean they established the home. And the home was an anchorage which meant, "We have come to stay. We have come and this is our land. This is where we are going to live out our lives and our children will live out their lives." A lot of stability can be attributed to the presence of women in the early Kentucky society. Think of the composite frontier woman in Kentucky society--on the trail, bearing children, administering to the sick, burying the dead, or building and outfitting the cabin, coming up with meals for the family, making do with what was there--all sorts of things--meeting shortages by substituting other materials. Think of the role that a woman played in all of that. She was "Johnny-at-the-switch" in the defense of Kentucky on many occasions. She stands out in the lives of Jemima Boone, the Callaway girls, or later on in the names of women like the Breckinridge, Hart, or Clay women, and so on to name some of the better known family groups.

Then, of course, you have the ante-bellum period where the more sophisticated Kentuckians began to put their women on pedestals, really denying them their rightful place in the functioning, decision-making society. The Kentucky woman of *Godey's Ladies Book* period or the glorified womanhood period became a pretty flaccid creature. That was not true of Kentucky women in general. We still had the activist woman on the farm or living in a small home, who was a strong personality in the making of that home and in the making of the community and the churches, and in the encouragement of the organization of schools.

After the Civil War, women became more and more aggressive; more and more a decisive factor in Kentucky society. In the 20th century, you began to have female leaders like the Breckinridges or Laura Clay or Mrs. Beauchamp, the temperance leader. You had Carrie Nation and women speaking out and more and more gaining privileges and a dignified place for women in Kentucky society.

Today, we have almost become a matriarchal state. We have a woman governor, a woman Superintendent of Public Instruction, we have women in the legislature, women in administrative offices all over the place. We have women presidents of colleges and universities. And I think that is only the tip of the iceberg. I think that as women become more numerous than men in this Kentucky society, it will become more and more a female dominated society.

B. C.: Would you say that Kentucky, although a rather conservative state, has been more liberal than most states in accepting women into the mainstream of public life?

T. C.: Yes. I think it would be safe to say that. I did not feel any earthquake tremors when Martha Layne Collins became governor. I did not feel the state quivering and sinking into a morass of confusion and conflict.

B. C.: Would this sense of equality possibly go back to the point you made of the frontier's rugged, dangerous nature, and that Kentucky's founding women were considered equal to men in those joint encounters with nature and Indians?

T. C.: I think so. I think they had that hard rock tradition. Also, I am going to make a statement that can be refuted in a minute. There are two sides to this coin, and I realize it. In the old agrarian subsistence farm history of Kentucky, a woman was just as vital in making a livelihood as a man. They worked right alongside of men in huge numbers in producing the materials of the family farm. In many cases, women were more aggressive figures than men. And that made transition easier. On the other hand, there was a large segment of Kentucky society in which women were highly sublimated to the male world and the male chauvanist--if you want to call it that. I always felt the term "chauvanism", which is being flung around so freely now, is not a very accurate or precise descriptive term. Women in Kentucky have been tremendously important. If I were a woman and went out crusading, I would crusade against that part of Kentucky's revered symbol of beautiful women. I would glorify women who got things done. And they do get things done.

A WOLF IN SHEEP'S CLOTHING

"Kentucky's educational system has been hampered from its beginning by forces which the state has been unable to overcome completely. There has been no desire to discourage education; quite to the contrary, Kentuckians have loved educational advantages and have on the whole patronized the best schools in the East. At home, however, they have had an inherent fear that public education was a wolf in sheep's clothing, and the history of public education in the state until more recent years has been a series of struggles and disappointments."

B. C.: I want to talk to you about education, and more especially teaching. Are we teaching history in the correct manner to our young people?

T. C.: I am, again, going to make some prefatory remarks about the teaching of history. Many times I have thought that maybe history should not be taught. Maybe it is something that should not be taken into the classroom. Yet, how would you create a historical sense in students without doing so? One of the great tragedies--and it would be hard for me to document this except what surveys over the past have indicated--is that history has been very poorly taught. A lot of times public schools are short on teachers. So they say, "Well, the coach may be able to read, so let's assign him history to teach." Or assign somebody on the assumption that he or she could teach. That prospective teacher most likely has had only one or two general history courses in college, and no matter how good the university professor is in teaching, all he or she can do is to distill out of a great volume of information some of the central facts and some of the central meaning and chronological developments. That is all he can do in a single introductory course. That's all there is time to do. These students have young minds, they have impatient minds. And they are not always sympathetic with the past. The history teacher has got to catch their attention in some way and he or she has to hope that they will leave a reasonable number of students with some glimmer of what it's all about.

Public schools "textbook" students to death. They drill them on textbooks, learning dates, learning trivial facts in a lot of cases. A lot of teachers have bored their students to death. I have had them say by scores, "I just hate history." They do not hate history--what they hate is the way it was presented to them or the method.

To be a good professor of history is a real challenge. I never went into the classroom, that before I stepped over the threshold I would say to myself, "God, let me get in and out of here without blundering and turning off student interest. Give me some magic with which I can capture their interest." I used to tell my students that history cannot be all spice--not all of life can be spice. You get up in the morning feeling bored and dull and you go through the day as a dull dummy. Societies have that same sort of experience. They have these down periods when not much happens. There is not much drama in the day-to-day operations when people behave themselves and the systems are working reasonably well.

There are some gimmicks which a good teacher can resort to. One is occasionally injecting personalities--biographical thumbnail sketches and relating them to the human experiences. The other thing is, you can once in a while inject a little humor. If you know some little anecdote about somebody, tell it. "General Jackson got into a hellofa mess accidentally." Tell them that. It's not significant in itself, but it relates them to the subject.

There was one thing in my own teaching--and I never changed my mind on this--I undertook to convince students that they were not very receptive at the youthful period right now as to the lessons of history. "You are young, you are growing," I'd tell them. "Your mind is focused on the future, not on the past. What are you going to do? Who are you going to marry? How big a family are you going to have? How much money are you going to make? Where are you going to live?" All these things are on their youthful minds. I would also say to them, "You are going to mature. You are going to get past the youthful stage. Reading will become tremendously important, and the older you get, the more inquiring you are going to be about the past. The past is going to be far more important to you."

And I never failed personally to emphasize the fact that for a person to say he is not interested in history is like some individual standing up and saying, "I'm not interested in fresh air." You have got to have some knowledge of the past to function in a society. Just think, if we ignored the past, where would our court system be? If we ignored personal history, where would our medical profession be? If we ignored the past, where would our religious institutions be? You could go up and down with every human institution, they all have a relationship to the past. It is a shrewd teacher who can some way or another plant in a student's mind this concept: "I am here on a chronological scale of mankind's development. I am here on this level, this is my level. Underneath me are all of these other levels, and this fellow down here on the bottom level was a very primitive man that lived by the most primitive means. The fellow on the next level had become a little more sophisticated, and all of these experiences, all of this knowledge, all of this business that's piled up behind us is our treasure."

We are the richest of all people that ever lived because we have not only our level on the chronological scale, but we have the advantage of claiming as our treasury storehouse all of mankind's experiences and knowledge. The great libraries, the great books, the great understanding of the mistakes that humans have made, the understanding of the great achievements that men have made, the understanding of the processes by which people have made decisions as they have gone along--to me that is what history is about.

B. C.: *Would you say that the biggest problem with young people, and I'm talking about the real young people, is their inability to relate those historical events to their day -to -day activity?*

T. C.: Yes. People can make some very, very foolish mistakes by not having the proper grounding in history, whether it be the history of a locality, the history of a county, or the state or nation or world system.

B. C.: *Is there a growing lack of an appreciation for history with our political leaders? Some historians even go so far as to say that John Kennedy was the last president to have a full appreciation and understanding of history. Do you find that governors, presidents and leaders, in general, of this country are having less and less appreciation of history?*

T. C.: And you see them making blunders.

B. C.: *When you read the speeches of the politicians of the past, including Stanley, you note that throughout their speeches they speak classicisms and historical interpretations, showing a real indepth understanding of history.*

T. C.: There's no doubt in my mind that many Kentucky governors have seemed to lack a mature knowledge of the history of our state. The history they know is sort of an applied thing, a glimmer. I have seen them come and go and they seemed to have had only limited knowledge. If you asked one of them to get up and speak on the history of the Commonwealth, I doubt that some could have done so effectively.

B. C.: *Do you agree with that assessment of national leaders as well?*

T. C.: Surely. There is no one who seems to be more oblivious to the historical past than Ronald Reagan. Oh, surely.

B. C.: In speechmaking by any politician, that deficiency is easily detected. What about in policy-making and decision-making?

T. C.: Well, it means everything. For the political leaders of the present, I pose these questions: "Do you all want to duplicate the mistakes you have made in the past that resulted in something disasterous happening? Do you want to go on, for convenience's sake, making that same decision, which is a process of re-inventing the wheel? Is there not some different approach? What are the facts? What are the conditions? What are the bearings in this situation?"

A knowledge of history would also be a guide to formulating a policy. With all the understanding and all the ramifications and experiences in the past, you can formulate a policy that will have a newness, a freshness, and an originality about it, but not be oblivious to what has gone on in the past. You do not want to make a damn fool of yourself by exposing your ignorance about the past.

Harry Truman had a very good sense of history. He was one of the best informed of the modern presidents on history. Of course, when you get back into the Adams--Jefferson--Monroe--and Madison era, those men were very well attuned to history. And then you come along to the Jacksonian commonherd and you make a departure in which the rabble gets into the picture. By saying rabble I am certainly not advocating an aristocracy, but I do believe that an informed citizenry is a very valuable thing to have around.

B. C.: Back to the methodology of teaching, it seems like we're falling into this rut of teaching American history chronologically from beginning to end. When we study American history, we automatically begin with Columbus discovering America, moving on to the development of Jamestown, and on and on up to the present time. I've never read a history book and I've never been in a history course where you went backwards, starting out with the current events and going back in history rather than forward. It would seem like that type of methodology would aid youngsters in relating the present to the past. Is there any support for that type of method?

T. C.: You know, I've sat in hundreds of hours of discussions of curriculum and the teaching of history. History is hard to teach. But, if you used that method, you would change the dynamics of progress.

I see nothing wrong with saying that this is the natural situation which you face in your age of history, and then going back and picking it up from the beginning and developing that idea and unfolding it right down to where you are at the present state.

But, you almost have to have that dynamic sense of human progress. If you got into a regressionary state, I do not know where you would go with that. You would be nowhere as a matter of fact.

I do want to touch upon the art of teaching history. Some of the things that teachers do don't amount to a damn. I have sat with historians over and over where they are just like lawyers and doctors and anybody who has a common cause or a common profession. We ask ourselves: What is it we are doing? What is it that a historian does? Is he a useless member of society? Does he serve society in some constructive way? The old conservative historians--the old classicists--will say that, "By George, he is not serving society. He's serving other historians. He is writing for other historians. He is writing and developing ideas and factual information. He is developing interpretations to enable future generations of historians to write other interpretations." I do not hold with that. Society has too big a stake in the historian--and should have. They must be very demanding of him, too.

Now, getting back to teaching. I know of a college teacher giving a course in early--maybe neo-classical, or classical history. His students are making Greek sausage. Now, his students, no doubt, are very interested in making Greek sausage. They get a sense of what the Greek people were eating, and what it tasted like, if the ingredients are correct. But, that doesn't tell you much, if anything, about the motivating forces and the changes and challenges of the age. Those things are like birth itself. They have to come the old fashioned way. You have to get out and dig them out and be able to identify significant facts when you find them.

B. C.: What advice would you give to the teacher who's dealing with the fidgety and restless fifth grader as to how to impart to him or her an appreciation, or even a reason, for paying attention to history?

T. C.: Generally, history at the fifth grade level would have to remain pretty much anecdotal. Give them the sense that there was somebody back there in the past, and that somebody put his breeches on one leg at a time, and he lived very much under human situations. The fifth grader can relate himself to elementary facts such as getting up in the morning and getting dressed, eating, reluctantly maybe, a breakfast. He can relate himself to that person in the past in simple physical ways. I would stick pretty much with anecdotes--I would not try to overburden the student with chronology and interpretive facts. I would not try to overload him with continuity. I wouldn't try to impress him very much with interpretations.

B. C.: Is there any reason why we settled on teaching Kentucky history in the lower grades?

T. C.: No. That question has come up many times. It ought to be taught up in the tenth or eleventh grades. Teach students at this level a little bit about the pioneers--early--and then get down to the nitty-gritty of discussing social, economic and political forces in the higher grades.

B. C.: Is Kentucky history taught very much in universities?

T. C.: Yes, it is taught. It isn't taught as much or as seriously as it ought to be. The University of Kentucky has been very lax in teaching it. There are historians who say state history has no significance and is clearly a local anecdotal thing. That is wrong, wrong, wrong. That is where ninety percent of the people live. In my book, local history can't be ignored. Locally, that's where people function as citizens. That is where the Bill of Rights resides. That is where the citizen casts his vote and that is where he exercises all his other rights. That is where he goes to court, where he sends his prisoners to the penitentiary or to jail, where he sends his patients to hospitals, and where he educates his children. There's every reason why local history is important. All those things are important.

B. C.: How could we, in your estimation, better prepare our history teachers?

T. C.: There are some people to whom you could give courses from now until judgment day, and they would be no better teachers. They might actually be worse teachers. For the average teacher, if I were going to prepare for him or her an ideal curriculum, I would put them on a pretty full reading diet. I would try to establish the best reading habits possible right at the start.

The second thing, I would make that reading selection a pretty broad one, going right back to the classics, back to the bedrock of learning. I would lay great stress on the methodology of research. Not that I would be trying to develop research historians--I would do that elsewhere. But, give the prospective teacher a sense of how you dig up and evaluate facts, and undertake to evaluate situations and make interpretations. Wrong as many of the pragmatic and empirical approaches might be, they do give a teacher a sense of how history is written and interpreted. That's the way you do it. I'd give them a sense of that. Then I would give them a sense of purpose--why are they teaching history and what the end objective must be. Too many historians are not very good at teaching methodology. They are not very effective in the art of pedagogy. Most of them now are the so-called "trained" historians who are specialized in areas. Sometimes I think that has been a bad intellectual animal that we have turned loose. The overtrained historian has placed all his emphasis on research and writing.

I grew up through the old "publish or perish" era, which is a damnable thing that functions in our academic system.

This is about the most simplistic statement that a man can make but I think a good history teacher in the classroom is born, to a large degree, and not made. You have to do a lot of making because he was born a pretty rough specimen, but personality and all those things figure heavily in the process of teaching. Teaching is a very challenging thing. When you think about your own college career, how many professors do you recall? I will bet not half a dozen. I suspect you would be hard pressed to say what some of them taught, or what they said in class. That has been the experience of almost everybody who ever went to school. Yet, there may have been one person--and he or she may have been the dullest person on the faculty--that had an impact on you. He or she said something one day in class or in a private conversation, or some way or other caught your attention. They didn't know how they did it--you didn't know how they did it--but they stimulated you, perhaps greatly motivated you. In my own teaching experience, I had a fear of blunting a student's interest in history. I tried to steer clear of the old chronological and bare factual approaches. To me, history has always been a vibrant and lively record of man and his responses to his environment and his times. So I tried to present it in this vein in my own classroom.

The classical influence on Kentucky is important and it has manifested itself in several forms. First of all, the old academies that were organized, such as Transylvania University had a classical curriculum.

B. C.: What are we talking about when we say "classical curriculum"?

T. C.: We are talking about a Latin and Greek emphasis up through the various stages of difficulty of reading Greek or reading Greek philosophy or any legend, and mythology, or Roman history. The old academies depended heavily on the classical curriculum. Transylvania's curriculum was made up almost purely of classical courses.

I do not hear it anymore, but I used to hear old-timers in Lexington talking about their lessons in Greek and Latin, and they said that was the only kind of education worth having--was the involvement in procuring an old classical or A. B. Degree.

In 1819 or 1820, when the Turks invaded Greece, and subsequently in the Greek revolution, the people in North America, generally became terribly wrought up over that revolution, supporting the Greeks in driving the Turks out of their country. There were all kinds of classical societies organized to support the Grecian cause.

When I was in Greece, I went to a good many of the old cities of the 1820's revolution. There were still strong feelings--monuments were all over the place--to the heroes of the revolt. American newspapers here were full of news about it. The societies stirred popular interest. I would not say that all Kentuckians even knew about the Greek revolution, but in the pockets where there was a little more sophisticated background, you had a classical interest.

Beginning with 1825, you had introduced into Kentucky a thing that made its mark on the state, and still does. It left its mark very definitely on the whole South. That was the introduction of Greek Revival architecture. Gideon Shryock studied architecture under William Strickland in Philadelphia and came back to Kentucky and introduced the Greek Revival in some public buildings which still stand. I think one of the best buildings in Kentucky is the old State Capitol in Frankfort. This is a marvelous old building. It is chaste in design and interior structure. Also the material from which the building is constructed is of classical texture. I have visited many a Greek temple and Greek ruin that is of no better design than the old Kentucky state house. You could put that building down in the heart of Athens and it would seem to be right at home. There is Morrison Chapel on the Transylvania University campus, also the Jefferson County Courthouse. Now, I don't want to over emphasize the latter because it has only a touch of true classicism. That structure has a long history of design and construction and

Thomas D. Clark, age one, 1904.

Sallie Bennett Clark, Tom's mother, 1904.

Cotton pickers in an exceedingly fine field of cotton, 1910. A familiar sight of Clark's childhood.

Young Tom Clark as right guard of the Choctaw Aggies, Weir, Miss., 1924.

Clark at the time he became an instructor in the University of Kentucky, 1931.

Dyonycious Clark and Alice Magee Bennett, maternal grandparents of Thomas D. Clark.

Thomas Whitfield Clark, paternal grandfather of Dr. Thomas D. Clark.

Scott's Springs Schoolhouse, circa 1917, the last elementary school Clark attended. His mother, Sallie Bennett Clark taught at the school which was located in Beat 4, Winston County, Mississippi, about two and a half miles from his home.

Clark's family at the Clark United Methodist Church sign in Anderson County, South Carolina, his ancestral home. From the right: Elizabeth T. Clark, Thomas D. Clark, Wilma Sanders, Irvin Clark, Emma Lee Clark, and Ethel Atkinson.

Main Street of the cotton town of Louisville, Mississippi at the time of Clark's birth, 1903.

Celebrating the end of World War I in front of the Methodist Church in Louisville, Mississippi, November 10, 1918.

1910, Main Street, Louisville, Mississippi. The mule drawn lumber wagons served the big lumber industry which was in full swing. The old fashioned false front store next to the Bank of Louisville was the J.D. Mcgraw General Store where Clark's family bought farm supplies.

Main Street as Clark knew it in 1916. The T-model Ford automobile had just become popular.

The Iron Bridge across the Tallehega Creek-- a community landmark. Clark went aboard a dredge boat in 1919 from this bridge to work for two years. His father's funeral procession was the last time the bridge was opened to traffic.

The dirt Main Street with the public well in the middle. The street is lined with cotton wagons. Circa 1905.

Culture came to Louisville, Mississippi in 1912. Four pianos were being delivered to the town. In the background is the L.B. Graham Hardware Store which was a community institution.

Clark and former Governor Bert T. Combs, 1982.

Clark and Colonel Harland Sanders. Colonel Sanders was speaking critically of the gravy served by Kentucky Fried Chicken, 1972.

Presenting Volume II of the *History of Indiana University* to Governor Edgar D. Whitcombe, Jr. of Indiana in the Governor's office, Indiana, 1973. Right to left: Thomas D. Clark, Claude Rich, David Dirge, acting president of Indiana University and Governor Whitcombe.

Speaking to the Kentucky Senate, 1984. Lt. Governor Steve Beshear presiding over the Senate.

Thomas D. Clark and Lt. Governor Steve Beshear, 1984.

Receiving fifty year certificate from Ray Hornback, University of Kentucky, 1929 class reunion, 1979.

Lexington Mayor Scotty Baesler and Clark at the 1982 dedication of the new Second National Bank building, East Main Street, Lexington, 1982.

Clark and Julius Hager, Director of Extension at the University of Kentucky, 1974.

Authors and former neighbors Thomas Clark and A. B. Guthrie, Jr., at the Frankfort Book Fair in 1985. Cleo Dawson Smith, author of *She Came to the Valley*, is in the background.

Four members of the Department of History of the University of Kentucky who had just published books. Right to left: Holman Hamilton, William Clement Eaton, James F. Hopkins, and Thomas D. Clark, 1963.

At Clark's desk in Frazee Hall, University of Kentucky, at the time of his retirement as Distinguished Professor in 1968.

Receiving the Gold Medal of Citizenship from the National Society of the Sons of the American Revolution, Louisville, Ky. September, 20, 1980.

Spindletop Hall, November, 1983. Left to right, Mary Wharton (back to camera), Clark, Earl Wallace, Sr. and Elizabeth Clark (back to camera).

In conversation with Mrs. Edward (Lucy) Prichard.

The Kentucky Oral History Commission, 1983. From the right: front row, Vivian Rousseau, John Ed Pearce, Kim Lady, Lynwood Montell. Back row, Robert Kinnaird, General William Buster, Thomas D. Clark, James Nelson, Lois Mateus, Dutch Ishmael.

Receiving the Sons of the American Revolution (S.A.R.) citizenship medal from professor John S.Herrick, 1980.

Clark in search of the Tennessee-Kentucky boundary in preparation of *Historic Maps of Kentucky*, Simpson County, 1978.

At the Charleston, West Virginia Authors Luncheon October 10, 1959. Left to right: Jean Thomas, Clark and Willie Snow Etheridge.

Clark, Mrs. Gloria Singletary and Elizabeth Turner Clark, at the Singletary's Stadium Luncheon, 1984.

Three Kentucky authors, J. Winston Coleman (back to camera), Thomas D. Clark, and C.V. Whitney, at a literary luncheon in the Lexington Public Library, 1975. (Reporter is from WLEX Television.)

Clark autographing Volume III of the *History of Indiana University,* Bloomington, 1975.

On the steps of Morrison Chapel, Transylvania University, discussing Kentucky education with Robert Sexton, Director of the Prichard Committee.

Thomas D. Clark, 1985.

Thomas D. Clark (photo by James Archambeault)

there is a lot of controversy connected with it. There was introduced the Greek Revival home. It became a mark of affluence, and still is--families living in the Greek temples with porticoes and columns had at least a physical mark of aristocracy. It may be a Georgian building on the back and a Greek classical building on the front. The classical era went a long way to set a level of taste and culture in this state.

B. C.: How did we acquire this Greek emphasis to the point even where Lexington was referred to as "The Athens of the West"?

T. C.: That is almost beside the point to what I am talking about here. Lexington got the designation of "Athens of the West" because of the location of those old classical academies and Transylvania in the town. It was the early hub of educational development here in Kentucky.

B. C.: Was this old Greek influence or the classical influence unique to Kentucky and Lexington?

T. C.: No. It spread throughout the South. There was the University of Virginia, for instance, with its modernized curriculum. After 1817 and 1818, you still had emphasis on the classics. In other universities and colleges throughout the South there was heavy emphasis on the classical curriculum. And just across the river at Indiana University, which was founded in 1819, its curriculum for years was largely based on the classics.

B. C.: Do you see a need or a place for the reintroduction of the classical curriculum in today's educational system?

T. C.: No, I do not. I think that such heavy emphasis on the classics has no great relevance. Now, after I've said that, I think it is terribly important for a sophisticated individual to have a background in Latin as the root of his language. The Latin root is so very important. I also think the sophisticated individual should have some understanding of Greek mythology and legends. Also, the Greek city states or political organization. All of these things--for instance, the drama--the Greek tragedy, the Greek theater are important. I think any educated person should have an understanding of these things. But to drill the old classical sense upon the modern twenty-first century student would have a high degree of irrelevance. Nevertheless, I want to emphasize again that it is important to know some Latin, and know something about origins of our mother tongue, the English language. I did not have a very good course in Latin, but I had enough to understand that it was basic to my understanding English. I had more Greek than Latin. Never did I think I would have any use for Greek. Had I known it was as interesting as it was, I would have taken Greek all the time I was in college. I never realized that there would come a time in my life when I would be thrown directly into contact with Greece and its people. Of course, there is a wide gap between speaking contemporary Greek and classical Greek.

WORKING IN THE VALE OF CONTRASTS

"**In the great vale of contrasts, Kentucky authors have** found characters in abundance with which to people their books, and situations enough to form an interminable number of plots. None, however, has produced the universal Kentucky story, nor has an author yet fathomed the deep recesses of the Kentucky tradition in the sense that mother Virginia has been portrayed in the novels of its authors, or in the biographies of its great men. The Kentucky story and society fall into parts which none so far has been clever enough to mold into a single piece."

B. C.: You have a reputation as not only a prolific writer but an interesting one as well. What kind of problems and frustrations do historians have in writing history in a readable form?

T. C.: I'll preface my answer to that question by saying I have always had a yearning in my heart to write "the" book. I don't think any author ever writes "the" book. There is always one out there somewhere that could be a lot better than the one he has written and have a lot more substance to it, be more polished and finished. It could be a lot of things and have better research behind it. Much of that comes as an afterview of a book. Once a book is published it becomes engraved in granite. There's not anything an author can do to recall it. It's out there and it exposes his virtues if he has any, and his weaknesses. It exposes his failure to be as comprehensive as he might have been, and all sorts of weaknesses may show up. And, of course, if he has any virtues, they will show up, too.

I would say to historians, generally, and young historians in particular, that I think the writing of history for the most part should be a literary undertaking. By that, I mean it should be clear, it should be simplistic in style, and at the same time it should be factual and objective. I have never seen any fault or had any objection to a historian adding color so long as he does it with subtle touches. Some historians will add a touch of humor, a touch of color, and wade in with a four-inch paint brush and dab it down. That, in my opinion, is not quite the way you do it. I imagine I have done some of that, though. I'm sure I have.

In all my teaching career, I have never been able to solve a mystery. I would sit at the typewriter or with a lapboard and work on a manuscript and get it written out in some fashion in a draft, and then I would take the draft to the typewriter and type it, and get it out as clean and clear as I could, and go at it again. I don't think I've ever had a book that hasn't gone through at least six or seven drafts, and that means a lot of work--a lot of paper and a lot of lonely nights. Writing is a lonely business, but I have from the start determined that what I wrote was going to have some style. If I had any capability at all, I was going to give it some style. And I must say, as I sit down and read the works of other historians, I come away feeling very humble. They are able to write into their works a great deal of soul and spirit and a great volume of factual material. They are able to give their works substance, and I stand back and envy them for being able to do that.

B. C.: Do other historians have such unique style that you, as a historian, can detect them right away? Could you take a historical work off the shelf without knowing who wrote it, read it, and say, "This sounds like ...."?

T. C.: No, no. That would be ridiculous to say that I could

do that.

I guess everybody has somebody who is a model for him. Ulrich B. Phillips in *Life and Labor in the Old South* and the book on slavery, and his essay, "Slavery: The Central Theme In Southern History", had a polished style. I read Phillips with great attentiveness. I did not read Charles Sydnor with the same interest. Sydnor wrote clearly, but he had a certain formality about his writing. He was so dedicated to fact and circumspection of interpretation that he didn't give you much margin in style to go on. There have been a lot of historians who have written with a flair and with a marvelous clarity of style.

It was tragic that Bernard Mayo did not finish his biography of Henry Clay. In the first volume of that projected work, there is a chapter called "Athens of the West" which is one of the nicest things that has ever been written about Kentucky history. It is beautifully written, yet it said everything that needed to be said so that the reader got everything he came for, plus a bonus in good writing style. I am not saying that style is everything. Style is important, however. I used to wonder how students could write a term paper and turn it in, dash it off in one round. I could not do that--they couldn't either very well, but the fact that they turned in anything amazed me. Sometimes I realized that they copied stuff, or they had help from some other sources. I never ceased to be amazed at that. Good writing is hard, sweaty work.

I was down at the University of Texas giving lectures, and I had a little time on my hands and I discovered in their very fine manuscript collection that they had a lot of Faulkner material that they had picked up somewhere. I went to look at it. Faulkner tore up his stuff--he ripped it up, transferred parts from one place in a manuscript to another, rewrote, crossed out, he just simply mangled a manuscript. Tom Wolfe needed to do the same thing, and did do much the same thing. The collection of his Houghton manuscripts in the Library at Harvard shows how harem-scarem he really was as a writer.

In my own writing, I have worked and worked and worked over manuscripts, and I think I have discovered something over the years. No matter how much you work, it all depends upon what kind of copy editor you draw. If you get a very demanding, meticulous copy editor, then he or she is going to mold you in his or her own image in a lot of cases. I let a copy editor make a mistake in a book once. But, for the most part, I've been lucky in the editors I have had. I have come away in the publication of a book very grateful to them for their contribution. In my *Southern Country Editor* book, I let the copy editor cut in too deep into my style. If I had it to do over again, I wouldn't let him do it. I would take the manuscript back and look at it myself and write it to the point I thought it should be written. I would just stand for a minimum of editing. That is a book that I have wished many times I could have kept the copy editor from cutting in too heavily.

For *The Kentucky* in the "Rivers of America Series", I had a marvelous editor. I never saw him. He must have been a marvelous writer himself, or at least I thought so. That editor, except for demanding that I reduce the volume, made no heavy demands on the text. That is one of the few manuscripts I have ever had where the copy editor used red ink. Copy editors usually do not write on a manuscript, or they will not write much on it. They have those little paste tabs and they will write notes on those calling your attention to questions or making suggestions. A lot of times you get back a manuscript with all those tabs pasted on it and you will think, "My Lord, they have just torn the manuscript to pieces." They, however, may not want to know anything but one word, or they may say, "Is this the right date?" or something like that. They have to have a tab for everything they put in. There are copy editors and there are copy editors. I read the reviews all the time and find books in which the reviewers are scolding the copy editors as much as the authors, and they should.

B. C.: What value do you think that fictional writers such as Faulkner and Thomas Wolfe have had in educating people as to history? Have they added to people's understanding of history, or have they diminished from it because of distortions that may have occurred in their writings?

T. C.: A novelist writes for the times. He is of the times that he writes about and he reflects the times. He reflects the public taste and what he believes to be the public interests. He reflects a second level in time context. If he's writing a historical novel, he's got to project himself into the past. He has to in some way crawl back in that tunnel of time and focus himself in that particular moment that he is writing about.

Let's take Faulkner, for instance. I knew him and worked on a golf course with him for three years. I don't know how broad and introspective of a view he had of the society around him. But, he almost took in with his mother's milk--as did most Mississippians of that time--a knowledge of a stratified society and of the goings and comings of individuals trying to survive in that social matrix of his age. That thing he called Yoknapatawpha County, I'm sure was in large measure Lafayette County, Mississippi. Everybody second guesses a novelist about his characters and the locale. But I think Faulkner was so clear in his locale that his famous county had to be in good part Lafayette. Or, it could have been any north Mississippi county. He wrote of people within social capsules, people who were of a social class unto themselves. In "The Barnburners", or in "The Bear", or in *Light in August*, or *Sanctuary*, he gave you a keen sense of the context of the time, of the social turning of the mind, or of the fabric of human life and values. He could not do that now. If it were possible to bring Faulkner back from the grave and say to him, "You sit down here and begin all over again and write about Yoknapatawpha", he couldn't do it. It vanished with him. He caught it right on time.

My neighbor wrote a Pulitzer Prize-winning book next door to my house. A. B. Guthrie wrote *The Way West* and *The Big Sky*, and a lot of this third book next door. I have a personal feeling and I knew these books right from the moment the first ink was put on paper. *The Big Sky* was a much more powerful book than *The Way West* and I am still of that opinion. *The Way West* is a little softer book, but the history in those books is first class. It is better history than a lot of historians of the west have written, because

Bud collected a very good library and he spent hours and hours poring over the historical sources. He had a big glass-topped work table and a map of the West under the glass. He would work over that glass with a black crayon so that when he said something about a place you could bet it was there. There was no fiction in that. The result is that I doubt anybody will supercede *The Big Sky* in catching the raw transitional phase from mountain man, from trapper, trailbreaker, breaking into the virgin land in the transitional period to the coming of settlers in *The Way West*. His intention was to write four books, which he did, *The Big Sky, The Way West, These Thousand Hills* and *The Last Valley*. He set out to write fictional accounts of the growth of the West from the time of the primitive trapper--hunter--Indian--land right up to the settlement of the land and the establishing of economic entities in the land. I know for a fact that his history is dependable. *The Virginian*, for instance, in spirit and in fact--I suppose the experience of *The Virginian* could not be duplicated. But Wister's book gave western history a dimension. It gave history a sense of the dynamics of an expanding west. It is hard sometimes for a historian to do this.

Now, a historian cannot write fiction and remain creditable. Every once in a while I have someone say to me, "Why don't you write a novel?" I can no more write poetry or a novel than I could fly. I would be lost trying to write dialogue or getting inside the minds of people and delivering their thoughts on paper. I am not trained to do that. My training has been to take a big volume of primary sources, get into an area where nobody's done much work on it, dig around and come up with some substance. I have always prided myself on being able to do that after some fashion.

B. C.: On balance, do you think the fictional novelist has contributed to the understanding of history?

T. C.: He has put a lot of icing on the cake. Yes, sometimes I find a good sound novelist can really give you a better sense of interpretation than a historian, because a novelist can present his material in human terms. He can translate his material in emotional terms and get inside the human psychic. A historian can't do that, he had better not do it. He's not a psychologist or a god. He can only go so long as he has that concrete foundation of documentary fact under his feet. The moment he steps off of that, he is on shaky ground.

B. C.: What were your personal impressions of William Faulkner?

T. C.: Faulkner was an interesting man. When I say I knew Faulkner, that does not mean I really knew him. I knew him walking around and helping me on the golf course at Ole Miss. I knew the little gray-haired man with ragged breeches. Some days he would come out to the golf course and be very talkative and very friendly.

B. C.: Where was this?

T. C.: University of Mississippi.

B. C.: What was he doing there at the time?

T. C.: He was not doing anything that was readily visible. He was just a plain fellow. Now, I am not quite honest with you in saying that. He had been postmaster and his father was a business manager of the university. His father, I suppose, had tried to help get Bill something to do, and he got him made postmaster. He was the most irresponsible postmaster I guess that was ever appointed by the United States Postal Service. Instead of sorting the mail, carefully putting the right letter in the right box, he gave everybody some mail. He would take a bundle of mail and put a few letters in every box, and let everybody be happy. Nobody would go look in his box and be disappointed.

When a patron would come up and look in his box he would say, "My, Lord, I have got a lot of mail in there today", but he would not have a thing. He had everybody else's mail chucked in his box. Well, the postal inspector got a little weary of those complaints and fired him. That is when Faulkner said he wasn't going "to be at the beck and call of every son-of-a-bitch with two cents in his pocket". Then he started working and playing on the golf course right after that happened. And, he had no means of making a living. As far as the people around Oxford were concerned, they called him "Count No Count"--he would wander around. That is how little the community knows of a writer. That is how little people can really gauge creative talent. That has been true a thousand times over. What Faulkner was doing, he was writing *Light in August*, or *Sanctuary*, or maybe "The Bear". I do not know, maybe "The Barnburners", any of those short stories.

Right after I left Ole Miss I went over to Chapel Hill on a visit to a former professor of English, A. P. Hudson, who knew Faulkner quite well. He was a professor at Ole Miss. The Hudsons had gone through hard times at Ole Miss and were just as poor as they could be because of very low salaries at that institution. They had been in Mississippi for ten or fifteen years and their salaries were very low. Hudson had been appointed head of the English Department by Theodore Bilbo and he refused to serve under those circumstances. He got the job at Chapel Hill. I went over from Duke University to see him, but he was not home. His wife invited me in and I sat down, and there was the *Atlantic Monthly*, which had a review of--I've forgotten which book--either *Light in August* or *Sanctuary* with Bill Faulkner's picture. If it had been the picture of that little Negro that had helped us out on the golf course, I couldn't have been any more startled than to see Bill Faulkner's picture in the *Atlantic Monthly*. Yet, that was the beginning of one of America's truly great writing careers. He was of one temperament as a fiction writer, but in reality quite another. But internally, I think many novelists work somewhat the same as historians. A fiction writer, as I understand it and as I have observed, is never freed of his subject. It is turning over inside of him all the time--that dialogue business is a constant challenge. He is saying it and saying it again, and again, and then he is getting his characters inside saying, "How would I feel emotionally and psychologically in this kind of a situation?" A historian does not have to do that, he had better not do it. Yet, a little of that understanding is very good for him--to understand the motives of men. Why do men respond to pressures? Or make the decisions that they do? Why do they make errors? You have at least to understand that much human psychology as a historian.

B. C.: Another southern writer that we haven't mentioned is Kentuckian Robert Penn Warren.

T. C.: Warren is an exceedingly able writer. He is more of an extrovert than Faulkner. I have known Warren for a long time, but certainly not well. I had a letter from him the other day. Warren is more perceptive of the realities of the world around him. Take *All the King's Men.* That is, in my opinion, one of the truly great books which has come out of the South. It is a penetrative book. It is one that caught the ball bouncing at the right moment in time. Warren was in Louisiana and I am sure he observed and heard much of Huey Long's deeds and misdeeds.

He and Cleanth Brooks were there together editing the *Southern Review,* and I suppose that nearly 24 hours a day they heard something about the Long shenanigans and, of course, *All the King's Men* turned out very well.

He has written a stirring epic piece that comes within this particular area of poetic writing--*Brothers To Dragon,* which is really a harsh piece of writing about the lunatic nephews of Thomas Jefferson. Warren is able to put that sort of thing into the context of human emotions. Boynton Merrill has written an excellent book on the same subject. Boynton Merrill could not do what Robert Penn Warren did in *Brothers To Dragon.* But at the same time he dealt as a historian with the same material in his area and did as highly capable a job as did Warren. Warren's historical narrative poem, in my opinion, will endure.

In *Night Rider* I think Warren had a lot of historical fact to go on that he had gathered around Guthrie when growing up. There was an awful lot of historical research that needed to be done on this subject. I imagine you feel the same way about it.

B. C.: Writers like Warren, Wolfe, Faulkner and Guthrie wrote fiction that was based on historical facts, yet, they were at liberty to make it turn and twist the way they wanted. There has been a lot of criticism of the fictional liberties taken with history recently, especially with television. A good screen writer can take a historical incident and make it fictional, close enough to facts, however, so the people who are watching it will think it's historically correct. Isn't there a danger to this blend?

T. C.: Yes. I think television in the area of history has delivered a badly mixed bag. Some of it is good, some of it gives you a sense of presence, but most of it is terrible. Most of it would be better off if it had never been shown.

I'll give you an example. I was teaching at the time the "Daniel Boone" series was shown. A lot of students would sit up, instead of going to the library and reading and getting at the facts of the case, and watch that trash and they would come the next morning and ask me what I thought about the last segment. I said, "If you ever ask me again what I think about that trash, I am going to take my roll book out and flunk you right here and now, because that indicates that you're too juvenile to be in a university class." Now the "Boone" series was a sorry show.

The West, for instance, in a big broad category, is way over-romanticized by the television people, all the way from the sorriest two-bit Saturday afternoon western on up. There are some things you cannot do on television. You cannot crawl around on all of those bends and turns with a camera and do all the things that a novelist or a poet can do. You have got some angles you have got to get around and you have got to be sharp and plausible in doing so. I think television has been a curse in interpreting the field of history, yet there have been some marvelous things done by the media.

B. C.: When students read the writings of Wolfe and Faulkner, for instance, do they not have trouble making a distinction between fact and fiction?

T. C.: One of the problems that I found in teaching was trying to get students to read. I was very anxious to get them to read even a limited amount of historical fiction. I thought it would lead to more serious reading. They would get a feel, an insight that they could not get otherwise, but I was always scared to death to assign fiction because that is the only thing they would read. They would not read non-fiction and get a factual perspective and insight. That always bothered me no end. A serious historian will read Faulkner. It gives him a sense of a place, a time, a social reaction that he cannot get readily anywhere else. The same thing is true of Warren's *All the King's Men*, or Guthrie's *The Way West*, or Owen Wister's *The Virginian*. You could go on and on naming titles.

Now there is an area of historical writing that has always proved fascinating to me. But I have let life creep up on me without doing this kind of book. I would have liked to have done a biography. I don't agree with some other historians who scoff at biographies. I am not one of those who feels that way. I feel biographies are tremendously important, even though they may have serious faults--the author is liable to get too close to his subject. He is apt to adopt some of his subject's weaknesses and prejudices and become so idolatrous that he ceases to be objective. I think a good biography has a very real historical meaning.

There is another limitation in biographical writing. It takes a skilled author to be able to take a central figure and interweave his personal experiences into the larger fabric of a historical or political movement and to have that individual stand out as a landmark human being of his or her time. It's difficult to do that and at the same time represent all the other human beings within a certain scope of time and place.

B. C.: If you were asked to write a biography of a Kentuckian, who would you choose to write about?

T. C.: At times I have had a desire to do a biography of John

Fox, Jr. Or one of George D. Prentice, former editor of the *Louisville Journal* would be exciting--so would a biography of A. O. Stanley.

B. C.: You have the ability and Mr. Bud Guthrie has the ability to transport people who have never left their community to other parts of their country and even to other times.

T. C.: Well, there is one thing in writing--it is hard work. I always sit at the typewriter when I am getting a manuscript in final form, thinking "Who is it out there, where are those eyes, those faces and those readers?" They can turn up in the most astonishing places and be the most astonishing persons. I never cease to marvel at that. Every author gets letters. He gets a curious variety of letters. For a current book, he will get letters from those who have read it, most of whom will be very pleased with the book, and some of them will catch him in an error somewhere or some will take a different point of view. Or some of them will just write you what they know about the subject just to tell you that they know something, too. I never cease to be amazed when I see where the letters come from and where that book has gone. The other day I got a phone call from a young woman saying that she wanted to bring her father by here. I never had seen her father, but I knew quite well who he was, and I knew his father, and his uncles, and many members of his family, but some way or other I had never met him. They came by and I autographed *The Greening of the South* for him as a result. He came by to speak to me--he had come from the same town that I did. And in the round he said, "You know, when I was in Memphis, I bought your book without knowing who you were." That really bothered me. I was born and raised right under his nose.

B. C.: How would you compare the social classes of Mississippi with those of Kentucky?

T. C.: The Mississippi Delta is a world unto itself. It begins in the lobby of the Peabody Hotel in Memphis and flows down to the mouth of the Yazoo River at Vicksburg. In that flood plain of the Mississippi Delta there is a very close, encapsulated society. A tremendous amount of exclusive social intercourse goes on in the Delta. But I do not come from that section. I come from hill country in Mississippi and those people are altogether different animals, socially speaking. We had limited social intercourse with the Delta people, nor they with us. We were not "big cotton", we did not owe the banks everything we hoped to make the next year. We were not that free-wheeling. We lived rather strictly within the protestant ethic, with limited cotton production, limited financial capabilities, with close-knit family and community ties. We were altogether different in social and economic outlook.

Socially, the Delta people compare to the Bluegrass aristocrats of Kentucky. The hill country Mississippi compares with other parts of Kentucky. When I go into the Eastern Kentucky mountains, I can communicate with those people. I can go down to Eddyville and Kuttawa, and those people are much like my own people down there--they speak the same idiom and have much the same dietary habits and tastes, the same folklore, and the same protestant ethic. There are no fundamental differences.

B. C: Who are some of the more influential Kentucky writers?

T. C.: There were two writers in Kentucky that influenced me in trying to understand the state. I still think they offer a lot in understanding the sectional differences, the discernment of social variances of people living within certain social sections and conditions. They were John Fox, Jr. and James Lane Allen. I think that James Lane Allen's books give you a sense of the nineteenth century Kentucky mind, a sense of being present throughout his pages. Allen was a geographically highly circumscribed man. He never got outside the Bluegrass. And when he undertook to get away from the land itself and got into that psychological and sociological business, he pretty well lost his bearing. But *The Bluegrass Region of Kentucky, The Bride and the*

Mistletoe, Mettle of the Pasture, and *The Reign of Law,* those books are in a way historical documents. They give a sense of time and a place and of human reaction to the social conditions that existed.

John Fox, Jr. was really a reporter at large. In his correspondence with R.C. Ballard Thruston, you get a picture of a man living within the context of a very primitive society. When progress began opening those tiny windows from the outside into Appalachia and bringing in the engineers and the coal industry, and the commercial development of the region, you begin to penetrate those isolated creeks and hollows.

In *The Little Shepherd of Kingdom Come,* you get a very good picture of that influx of the pioneer stock that came into those hollows and ravines behind those big, black mountains of the Pine Mountain Range, and becoming land-locked there--the thing that Ellsworth Huntington called "contemporary ancestors". Fox caught those people right at that moment of change. It is just like going out here and taking a photograph. You can go out with a camera one minute and snap it and all you get is just a commonplace picture. But there might be something dramatic happening the next moment that you snap the camera and you capture the picture of a lifetime. That is what happened in Fox's writing. Fox is not a great novelist, there's no way of proclaiming his novels great. They are good documentary novels, documenting in spirit, providing a sense of time and place you normally cannot get. No matter how hard a modern author might try to write about Harlan County, or Leslie or Letcher Counties, you cannot do it in the vein of Fox's writings because the scene has changed so drastically.

I found Allen's and Fox's books very fascinating. I remember one time I took an essay down to Otto Rothpert, who was editor of the *Filson Club History Quarterly,* and he read it. Uncle Otto, as we called him, was never a man who would say, "This is a good essay", or "This is acceptable." He would never say that. He would always find fault and fuss at you about it. I remember once he said, "You ought to go back and read James Lane Allen with a great deal more care." He was stylistically speaking in this instance.

We produced, here in Kentucky, some writers in the past who are landmark craftsmen. I don't care what you say about Irvin Cobb, one way or the other. He left a good solid imprint with his humor, in his catching just that casual or folksy bit of humorous nature in his writings. Sometimes he went pretty far out to be humorous. He painted with a strong brush, but Cobb made a contribution. One of the areas that I feel where he made a contribution was by calling attention to his section of the state, and giving it both a literary flavor and push.

Another author that I think was of major consequence was Annie Fellows Johnston. Her stories are pretty insipid, but even so, look at what that woman did to a nation of readers. The older generation of women and girls all knew about Annie Fellows Johnston. That same thing goes for Alice Hegan Rice. I think the cabbage patch stories are superficial, yet that is perhaps very poor judgment on my part. Those books had an impact on Kentucky. This author wrote about a section and time in an urban setting. Hardly a year goes by that you don't read a feature story about Alice Hegan Rice. The University Press of Kentucky has republished one or two of her books, I think. You have to take those things into consideration.

Here in Lexington, in a later period, we had a lawyer-author who had a wonderful style. He was one of the most magnificent story-tellers I've ever known. William H. Townsend wrote *Lincoln and His Wife's Hometown*, *Lincoln and Liquor*, and *Lincoln the Litigant*. He contributed heavily to William E. Barton's unfinished biography of Lincoln, and other books. Bill Townsend had a marvelous style. He was an intimate friend of mine. He always said, jokingly, "Never let facts stand in the way of telling a good story." My how that man could write. His imagination worked overtime.

B. C.: He was probably the most influential person in bringing to public light the life of Cassius Marcellus Clay.

T. C.: Quite. He made that recorded speech before the Chicago Civil War Round Table--about three-fourths of that is pure Townsend, but it is marvelous. That is history as it ought to have happened, but it did not always. I went with Bill one afternoon over to Judge Shackelford's court in Richmond and I am positive as I can be that Bill was never back in the Judge's court again. Yet, he quotes that report of the Sheriff Posse Comatosc. I'm sure he made that up. It is too perfect. That is the way Bill thought it ought to have happened.

We have other writers--take Jesse Stuart. Whatever you may think about Jesse Stuart, pro or con--and Jesse was in an area where there were a lot of pros and cons--he made his mark in American writing. A good editor could take all that author's voluminous writing and condense it in a greatly reduced form and have a monumental literary contribution. Jesse wrote a lot of trash--all authors write some trash. They cannot very well avoid it unless something is wrong with them. He showed me one time, in a room in his house, what must have been 300 rejected manuscripts. Most authors try to keep those hidden to keep people from seeing them.

An author died the other day who was one of Kentucky's very best. She had a tremendous impact on an aspect of this state's social history. Harriette Arnow, who wrote *The Dollmaker*, and the marvelous books, *The Flowering of the Cumberland, Seedtime on the Cumberland, Hunter's Horn, Mountain Path,* and *Old Burnside.* Harriette Arnow in *The Dollmaker* came close to writing "the" classic book. That book will live so long as there remains the social and economic movement of people, and frustrations and the emotional and physical displacement of human beings. *The Dollmaker* will always be a valid book.

Janice Holt Giles was a successful and prolific author. She and her husband moved into a log house somewhere in the neighborhood of Glasgow or Scottsville. She wrote ably of that western part of the state. In Eastern Kentucky on the Ohio River, Elizabeth Chevalier wrote *Drivin' Woman.* I am sure you've read this book. It is about the tobacco war and the burley belt along the Ohio. It is a good book, too. It is a novel, but at the same time it gets so close to the facts of the tobacco unrest that you get a sense of what was happening.

Now, we would be poorer without these folks. One other author that I must mention and who has left a mark on American literature, and that is Elizabeth Madox Roberts. *The Great Meadow, The Time of Man*, and her *Black Is My True Love's Hair* are important. Those books are part of a rich folk culture. They are special literary resources of Kentucky. They are some of the "money in the bank" assets of Kentucky as a cultivated society. We have young authors that have come along and have done well indeed. I am not even going to begin to try to mention them because I do not know all their names off hand. Wendell Berry, for instance, has caught on. I imagine anything that he writes now would find a ready publisher. Harry Caudill has succeeded mightily with his writing. I believe Boynton Merrill is going places. He's certainly an intelligent man and he is well enough off that he can give time to his writing.

Gurney Norman, Ed McClanahan, and Charles Braceland Flood are mature authors who have attracted a national readership. No Kentucky author has exceeded James Still in talent and spirit in his writing. Of course, there are many other talented authors who deserve more mention than time and space permit. Kentucky is rich in writing talent.

B. C.: What aspect of Kentucky life do you feel needs to be written about more and has not been adequately illuminated either by current contemporary writers or past authors?

T. C.: There are several areas that should be written about and written about perceptively. I do not know whether I am factually correct or just emotionally hooked on this subject. Kentucky's undergoing a fundamental revolution. It has never been in a revolutionary state such as it is in right now. The old world agrarian way of life that it has lived by and cherished so heartily is rapidly disappearing. The times are developing a curious kind of pseudo-urban society which the Census Bureau calls a "rural non-farm population"--people who live in the country but have jobs in town. They are reluctant to give up the country. They do not want to become part of an urban industrial society. Early in the morning the roads around Lexington and Louisville are lined with hundreds of cars coming in from the rural non-farm population. A novelist could take this and do wonders with it, and a social historian could make a major contribution in catching this state in a moment when it is in such a revolutionary transition. It is subtle, you don't hear it roaring anywhere, you do not find people running out in the streets shouting about it everywhere, but you do see them in the streets. In the big shopping malls, look at the tags on the cars and see where they come from. They are from all over creation. Down around Calvert City or Russellville or Bowling Green at the Corvette plant. Or anywhere that you have an industrial plant you have a disruption of the old agrarian way of life.

The agrarian institutions have either disappeared or are rapidly disappearing. There is not anything approaching the old country school any more in Kentucky--not in the true sense. That was an institution that was one part education, two parts social. It was a social focus of a community. It was also a monument of pride for the community. Once the community lost its school it lost an enormously important centralizing force.

The country stores are another example. We still have country stores, hundreds of them, but we do not have the old general store where you could buy a barrel of flour or a horse collar, or any thing else in between. Those things have given way to the chain stores that are out peddling groceries, a few patent medicines, and maybe a few little dry goods. The dry goods stores have given way to the discount stores and to the big chain stores.

Many of the country churches have folded because their congregations have moved away. Every time one of these things happen, that is a decentralizing influence. Look at the third and fourth-class post offices that have been closed in Kentucky. There's a great story lying out there. That is what I mean when I say the time is right for catching certain things in a state of disappearing institutions. Now, you catch the people on the move looking for non-farm, non-urban jobs and a non-urban way of life. Each decennial census indicates that these changes are becoming more important. Pretty soon they will be equal to the urban population. They will surpass the rural farm population, if they have not already done so.

There is a book to be written along the lines of Harriette Arnow's *Seed Time on The Cumberland*. What seeds were planted early in Kentucky which have resulted in this state of revolution in the closing decades of the twentieth century and an inferior school system or other low achievements? What seeds of conservatism were planted back there which now make people almost impervious to change and the need of meeting challenges of the future--a fear of change that might come in the future? There's a good book lying in those questions. And in the agricultural areas we need a history of agriculture. That has been a way of life in Kentucky. There is a tremendously interesting story there. A good historian could take that and make it dance with meaning--he could make it readable and meaningful and make it contributory to an understanding of the state. That same thing goes for tobacco. If there ever was a time that a crop and an industry cried out for a historian, tobacco does right now. If you don't get it right now, some of it you're not going to be able to recover, because it is disappearing.

B. C.: What do you think, from your perspective as a historian, will happen to all those people that have received their sustenance from tobacco?

T. C.: I cannot answer that question with any factual certainty. Three or four things will happen to them. Those who have high school educations and have some skills and some capacity to make an adaptation will find industrial employment in the new industries that have come along, provided Kentucky can attract enough of those to meet the demands of its labor market. Those who do not have high school training and those who are satisfied doing heavy physical labor--the crude everyday farm labor, mining, or road-work or whatever heavy manual labor you have, they are going to be in a very rough situation. Mechanization has already displaced hundreds or maybe thousands of them. You are almost going to develop here a congenital or hereditary food-stamp or welfare situation. There's not much place else for untrained people to go. We're into the second generation, and in some cases, the third generation of welfare existence. If the social prophets are correct, these people simply can't compete with what's coming up in the twenty-first century in American society.

I think the big question in the minds of thoughtful people is: What is going to happen when you dig out all the coal? For instance, you read about the story of the big strip-mining machine at Peabody Coal Company. It was too expensive for them to dismantle and move when they had exhausted the coal supply. They just put it in a pit and buried it. That was the cheapest way to get rid of it. You have some counties in Eastern Kentucky that are coming, sometime in the forseeable future, to the exhaustion of their richest coal veins. They will have left behind the stripped land and unemployed people.

I have lived through a transition of a crop system. I remember vividly as a young boy when the boll weevil first came to the cotton fields in Mississippi. But I lived long enough to make a cotton crop myself in 1925 to get money enough to go to Ole Miss. That was just about the last good crop year as far as the little farmer was concerned. From that time on he became a vanishing animal. He no longer exists there. I have grand-nephews and nieces who could not identify a cotton stalk any more than a child from New York City could do so. If they have ever seen one, I doubt they knew what it was. Yet, children in my generation lived off the stuff. That is the way you made a living. It was a central part of our lives. What happened then--and I don't know whether this could possibly happen to Kentucky--the land was turned to pasturage and a tremendous change came in the livestock industry. Then they had to combat the screw worm and the Texas fever tick. Kentucky hasn't had the screw worm or fever tick that I know anything about. Kentucky has been in the livestock business from its beginning, but even it has its very serious limitations. I think a man would be pretty irrational to run out and buy a farm and say, "I'm going into the cattle business tomorrow."

He would be pretty foolish to do that without more serious planning.

B. C.: What biographies need to be written?

T. C.: I think the time has come when we should have some biographies of various people, going back into the early period. I think it would be very interesting to have a biography of Charles Morehead, who was governor in a somewhat sentimental period in the state.

I will just list at random the names that occur. The time has come for the writing of a really good biography of Harriette Arnow, getting behind the social forces and the social changes which went through her emotional system as a writer. Some time in the near future, maybe not right at the moment, I think a good understanding biography of publisher Barry Bingham should be written. There is a good political biography of Bert Combs that is on its way from John Ed Pearce that deals with Clements, Combs, and others.

We need to write the biography of some businessmen and maybe some major coal operators, not because we want to glorify them personally, but as personal actors in Kentucky's economic history. Harry Caudill in *Their's Be the Power* deals with a lot of these types of people. The story of John C. C. Mayo, for instance, would be a good biography.

Down in Western Kentucky, I think maybe a good interpretative biography of Alben Barkley and his times should be written. We are getting far enough away from Barkley now that a good evaluative biography can be written.

I would like to see a biography of A. O. Stanley. Stanley was in the World War I period and a time when heavy challenges were made on the governor's offices, and on the state and on the nation. He was a central figure in Kentucky.

I think a good biography of Augustus Willson would be useful. Not that he was a great governor or statesman. Nevertheless, he served in troublesome times, as you know.

The time has come for a good solid set of biographies of

educational leaders. Now whether their leadership was valid or not is another matter. The weaknesses and strengths of leadership is not significant in this area. There was a tremendous amount of weaknesses and there were a lot of strengths. I think we need to pick out certain key persons in the growth of the educational system in Kentucky and to write about them. There have been some university professors in this state who have made some important contributions. Take, for instance, my colleague in tobacco, W. D. Valleau. I knew him quite well. I had a tremendous respect for him. He did all that work in combatting nematodes and other infectious problems of tobacco. He saved the tobacco business. A good brief biography of a man like that would make a real contribution.

You had professors who taught students and had a real impact on this state through the trained people that they turned out. I am not just talking about the University of Kentucky. I am saying wherever you find them. There are those quiet men and women who have done yeoman service far beyond anything they were ever paid for and far beyond the call of duty.

B. C.: What is your assessment, Dr. Clark, of the role of a professor as a writer and the demands made upon him as a writer?

T. C.: I came out of graduate school in a period when things were beginning to heat up a bit in the South--up to mid 1920's, remarkably few southern university professors had written and published anything. That was not a requirement of their jobs. After the late 1920's, however, professors rather generally began to develop a profound interest in writing and research, especially in the area of regional history. However, that also spilled over into the area of non-American history--European and English history, especially. By the mid 1930's, there was a great deal of the "publish or perish" business that had crept into the southern universities--the organization of the Southern Historical Association had been a stimulus.

I remember going to the early professional meetings, and everybody was asking everybody else, "What are you writing? What kind of research are you doing?" The university presses were being organized. New channels of publications were being opened. I do not think the University of Kentucky ever--I do not remember any pressure ever being applied to me personally to be an active research historian. I did not really need it because I was motivated that way anyhow. I came out of graduate school well motivated in the research area. The University of Kentucky in those days did not have the library to support a professor to do a whole lot of research on the grounds. As a matter of fact, he could not do any of an appreciable quality. It was necessary for him to go away.

In that 1930's period, I published two books, *The Beginning of the L & N* and *A Pioneer Southern Railroad, Cairo to New Orleans*. One was published by the Standard Printing Company in Louisville and the other by the University of North Carolina Press. I did not know I was going to publish *The Beginning of the L & N*. That was an accident. Mr. D. B. G. Rose, who was very anxious to get business out of the L & N, got hold of a paper I had read at the Filson Club, and decided that he would make a book out of it. That caught me by surprise. I turned away from that railroad business after publishing the *Southern Railroad* in 1936. My interests turned into two areas. One was the history of Kentucky. I started back in 1933 with the preparation of the writing of *A History of Kentucky*. Between 1933 and 1937 I wrote and published that book, which became a standard text in Kentucky history, and still is, after all these years. It has been through six printings, but I do not intend to take it to another printing. I am through with it. I do regret that I am not young enough to start all over again and write a multi-volume history of Kentucky. I would love to do that, but that is too arduous a task, and I do not have time enough left to get that job done.

Once I got the Kentucky history out of the way, I became deeply interested in the frontiersmen. Despite all their hardships, the tragedies of war, and accidents which are simply a natural part of breaking into a new country, they had a keen sense of humor about it all. I got a bee in my bonnet to write a book about humor.

I went to work gathering the materials for the book, *The Rampaging Frontier*. In the research for that book, I discovered that wonderful periodical, *The Spirit of the Times,* in which William T. Porter, the editor, had a keen eye and ear for the humor of the frontier. I published that book in 1940, I believe, and I had good luck with it. It got good reviews. One of the first reviews I saw was by Bernard DeVoto in the old *Brooklyn Eagle*. A girl called me from the university library and said, "There's a review of your book in the *Brooklyn Eagle,* and I asked her if it was a good review or not, and she said, "Well, not so good." I asked her who reviewed it and she said, "Bernard DeVoto." I went over with fear and trembling because he could skin an author. He could tear a book to pieces and I thought that is what he's done to me. When I got there and read the review, it was wonderful. I do not know how that girl had arrived at the conclusion that it was not good.

Then, there began to appear the first volumes of the "Rivers of America Series". Constance Lindsay Skinner, the editor, said she was not going to use historians as authors. She was under contract with Farrar and Rinehart to edit the series. I came to know Constance Rourke when she came to Lexington to do research for the book *American Culture*. She died before she could finish it. I drove her around a lot and one day we were crossing the Kentucky River and I said, "I would give anything to be able to write *The Kentucky* in the "River Series". And she told me, "If you want to write it, I will write Farrar and Rinehart on your behalf and tell them that you should write *The Kentucky*." She did and I had a letter from John Farrar asking me to send him a copy of *The Rampaging Frontier*. I did, and he turned it over to Stephen Vincent Binet to review. I received a copy of the review from John, and it was a very favorable one, and in the same letter was a contract to do *The Kentucky*.

By that time I had pretty well established myself. With the *History of Kentucky*, the two railroad books, *The Rampaging Frontier*, and the river book under my belt, I had a pretty good foundation to go on.

There was a great deal of discussion back in those days about sharecropping and the failing system of southern agriculture. There was published in the "New Deal" days a yellow-backed pamphlet called, *The South, The Economic Problem Number One.* That thing stimulated a tremendous amount of discussion and controversy. There also had appeared that three volume work of fiction by Thomas Stribling, *The Store, The Forge, and The Unfinished Cathedral.* I read those books with a great deal of interest, and there were others coming out on the South. There had appeared a book called *Ninety Degrees in the Shade* , by Clarence Cason, down at the University of Alabama. I had correspondence with Cason. In fact, I had a letter from him just before he committed suicide. As you possibly know, he committed suicide before his book appeared. I have intended to go back and read it. It was a critical book of the old southern system--the landlord, the tenant and the credit system. It took in everything else in its swing, especially the Tom Heflin type of politics. Cason was afraid that he was going to be criticized so bitterly for it that he took his life. I never did know all the surrounding circumstances.

I felt that now was the time to get out and do some research and writing about the old financial system, or the old financing and tenant system by the old line general store, an institution which no longer exists. In the fall of 1941, I took my family down to South Carolina. We rented our house in Lexington to Frank Peterson who had become vice-president of the university. I left my wife and children with her family, and I set off across the South to gather material for the book on the country store. The first store I went to was an abandoned operation, and the records were scattered all over the floor and on the empty shelves. The former storekeeper gave them to me. There were some very interesting letters in that collection of papers. One was from James Byrnes, who was then U. S. Secretary of State, but much earlier he had wrtten the storekeeper when he was running for Congress asking him to exert his influence in his behalf.

The second store that I visited was a very interesting old place. It was out of business and the fellow gave me a lot of the records of that store. By the time I got to Athens, Georgia, I had so many business store records that I was about to break my car down. I deposited at the University of Georgia with a friend of mine, Merton Coulter, a carload of records, and I went beyond Atlanta and across Alabama, across Mississippi, over into Louisiana, and then I worked my way back. I had stored in Atlanta a big cache of records, and in Athens a bunch of records. I made a foray into Tennessee and came up to Union City and up to a little place--I've forgotten the name of that little town--where I picked up some records and hauled them back to Nashville. I went back to a brief research appointment I had at Vanderbilt University. I hauled back to Nashville a whole trailer load of records.

On Pearl Harbor Day, along the way, from Union City to Nashville, people were excited. Every place I passed through, they were talking excitedly. I wondered, "What is going on? What's all this excitement?" I did not know until I got back to Nashville that the Japanese had bombed the fleet at Pearl Harbor. I spent the first year of World War II doing research there at Vanderbilt and elsewhere in the South. I was appointed the head of the Department of History while I was gone that year of 1941. I spent the war years teaching soldiers and writing on my book, *Pills, Petticoats and Plows*. When it was published, it received wonderful reviews. It got a full page in *The New York Times*, and the New York *Herald Tribune*, and the Chicago *Tribune*.

B. C.: Who published that book?

T. C.: The Bobbs-Merrill Company of Indianapolis. It was a best seller for a brief period. That book brought me a lot of joy, indeed.

Then I set out to do a second book on the rural South, *The Southern Country Editor*. I have often mentioned that a copy editor can influence the form of a book. I allowed the copy editor to injure that book. I have always been sorry for that.

In 1948, by the time *The Southern Country Editor* was

published, there were no more immediate promotions in my future. I did not have anything at stake professionally. I had my reputation at stake, of course, but no promotions or anything of that sort. Now I never felt the pressure of the "publish or perish" syndrome. As I said earlier, I was self-motivated. I wrote because I wanted to write. I did research because I wanted to do it for the sake of growing intellectually--I found it exciting. However, by the latter part of the 1940's and the 1950's, the pressure had become pretty impressive at the university that the professors produce something. A lot of shallow books and articles were produced in that period, and still are, because it is still a "publish or perish" business. Every professional historical journal that appears has long book review sections. Many books are produced with the expectations of the author that he or she will get some professional advancement out of it. He or she did not necessarily write that book from just a pure joy of creative writing, creative production or expectation of monetary returns.

I sat and listened throughout my whole career to the argument about whether publication, research, and writing had any relevance whatsoever to a good teaching career. I was out of patience with that idea then, and still am. I think that just research and writing alone does not make a good teacher. If you are not a good teacher already, that is not going to help you much one way or the other. Except in this way--a man or woman who is doing research and writing will come up with a lot of original material and ideas, and that is important. Not only that, but he or she gains more than an ordinary textbook knowledge of some areas of their chosen field of interests. If they maintain a career of writing and publication, then, of course, they have tremendous potential for growth. Likewise, they have a bright potential for being a good teacher. I personally feel that it would be hard to be a historian--I do not see how you could be a successful historian--without having done three things. First, research under scientific and careful supervision. Secondly, research on your own where you are supposed to be mature enough to take a research project and see it through to completion. I do not see how a scholar could be thoroughly organized until he or she has had the responsibility for organizing research notes and putting them into mature text of some sort. Then, thirdly, in the writing of almost any sort of book in the field of history, you have to do a lot of reading. You have to come up with a lot of perspective.

I think--and I'm speaking of historians--they learn something about historical criticism that is vital--how do you find information, how do you exploit it, how do you organize it, how do you present it, what are the pitfalls, and what are the dangers? Once I heard a colleague of mine criticize another colleague--really he was laughing about him. He had just read a critical review of this fellow's book and I knew the boy was being critical. He had never published a book. Until you have gone before the public, naked and defenseless, to face the reviewers where they can say anything about you, then you do not have much right to giggle about an unpleasant review. That is the acid test--going through that final stage with the reviewers.

Now, to answer the question that I raised, "does research and writing aid teaching?" Yes sir. It gives you a certainty about things. It gives you a perspective about the whole business of historical criticism and historical evaluation. It develops a critical eye. Finally, research can be humbling in that it reveals how little you really knew about a subject.

I have always felt, in my own teaching, that I have profited greatly from my research and writing. Without writing, I never would have had two very precious experiences. One was the thrill and the exhilaration of making discoveries, of turning up some information that had never been used before and throwing some light on a subject that had some significance. The other, I felt that when I got into the classroom I could add an extra element of interest to the subject in hand, because I had a better understanding of the interpretation and the application of criticism that I never could have gotten without research and writing.

Finally, I think it is tremendously important for a scholar to have that harrowing experience of being reviewed. It's rough on him at times. No man has ever published a book that somebody did not jump on him about oversights and misjudgments. I have gotten to the point where I can take that just like walking down a road. Nevertheless, I know the critics are out there, and more often than not they are right. I am a great believer in a professor having organized a body of material and presenting it with as much maturity as possible. It makes him or her a better organized teacher than they otherwise would be. I do not think much of just the "publish or perish" idea--that gets to be pretty superficial.

REFLECTIONS

"**No longer do Kentuckians think of their land as the** garden. Time has gone almost too fast for Kentucky in the latter decades of the twentieth century. Changes have come so rapidly and fiercely for the stand pat traditionalists that they have come to feel themselves aliens within their native land. The ledger book no doubt stands about equally balanced between desirable and undesirable changes. In the great crusade to supplant the old agrarian economic base with industry, the whole social pattern has been uprooted.

There are indeed few islands left where some antediluvian Kentuckians can sit and cogitate the wonders of their small world. There are, however, a few country stores remaining which still furnish enough battered chairs, boxes, and benches for the accommodation of the vanishing ranks of wisemen whose minds function best amidst the fumes of tobacco smoke and neighborhood banter. A few remote country courthouse towns still line their squares with benches where less hurried citizens can find a seat and something to whittle on and even spit on the sidewalk without stirring social turmoil. These are the last strongholds of the old civilization; the main thrust of modern Kentucky is in another vein."

B.C.: Do you still miss the classroom and teaching?

T.C.: You know, in a period of 40 years, actually 43 years,

teaching here in Kentucky, and then 6 years more teaching in Indiana University, you have a lot of students. I had large classes. I calculated one time, the best that I could, the number of students I had had at the University of Kentucky and it ran to around 25,000. That is a lot of Kentuckians scattered out there somewhere--God knows where they are. They have gone everywhere. I get letters from some of them occasionally. I had a letter the other day from a boy in Maine whom I knew quite well. He was ill, and I went out to the Julius Marks Sanitarium a lot of times to take him books and keep him up with his course.

You asked me if I missed the classroom. I did at first. If you live about 49 years of your life regimented and scheduled by bells, you'd miss that ringing on schedule. In retirement you have to be careful about planning ahead of time what you are going to do or you will waste away all your time. In 49 years of standing in the classroom, I felt that I had had the most wonderful experience that a human being could have. I sometimes miss the classroom--I miss the give and take of the students, and sometimes I might have had the tendency to feel sorry for myself that I no longer had the privilege of going in the classroom and no longer had students or a roll book or had to listen to a bell ringing in my ears. Anytime I get to feeling sorry for myself I think about all those students that I have had, and they are out there. A host of them have succeeded. I can scarcely go out anywhere that I do not meet an old student. Over and over and over they come up and speak to me. I do not always know who they are, but if they will tell me, especially if they are girls--girls have a tendency to change more than boys--if they will tell their maiden names, I have a pretty good memory for names and I can many times remember having had them in class.

You know those people have done well. I hear a lot of criticism, continuous criticism about the school system, of universities and teaching, and I am sure much of it is merited. I am sure that we did not do all we should have done, perhaps, and I am sure that our successors have not improved on us to a marked degree. Teaching is difficult under any circumstances. But you know, you do more in teaching than you think you do. You plant seeds that sprout and materialize. I have the richest thing in Kentucky in the knowledge that so many students I had in class have done well. They have done well not in just an everyday sense, but they have succeeded in higher office--Ned Breathitt, for instance, as governor.

B. C.: Was he a student of yours?

T. C.: Yes. I have had judges, lawyers almost by the busload, bankers, and teachers all over the place. The greater number of students that I have had, have done exceptionally well. I had one boy who is now a national authority in the field of military history--Edward Coffman from Hopkinsville.

B. C.: Is Forest Pogue one of your former students?

T. C.: Forest Pogue, no. He received that little $200 scholarship in 1929-1930. He came here the year after I had that scholarship. Forest is a very able fellow and he has done exceedingly well. He has written a capital biography of General George Marshall. He told me the other day that he has just completed the final volume. He has a national reputation, a solid national reputation.

B. C.: Do you have any memorable antecdotes or experiences as a teacher that stand out?

T. C.: Oh, sometimes teaching can get to be a comedy of errors. I remember some things that are mildly antecdotal. One time I had a class that I was just so exasperated with. Its members did not seem to have enough inclination to come in out of the rain. I thought I would try them on simple geography. I wondered, " How much geography do these folks know?" I pretty well determined right at the onset that they did not know any. I went around the class and hammered them over the head with elementary questions and got nowhere, and in exasperation I said, "How in the world did you folks get to college?" A halfback on the football team spoke up and said, "There's one thing certain. We didn't come by river." He never would have found his way into the university if he had.

Sometimes old students will recall incidents that I know did not happen quite that way. And many times I see an old student that will remind me of something that had happened, and they have over the years done a right considerable amount of exaggeration. That is how professors get cranky reputations, by students enlarging on what really happened.

I had a big basketball player in class who came to the university from Indianapolis. He knew just one thing in this world and that was how to throw a basketball through a hoop. That is the only thing I ever detected that he knew or cared about. One day one of my colleagues came in and said, "I've a boy in my class who doesn't belong there, but I can't determine where he does belong. It sounds to me like he belongs in one of your classes." We began looking at his record and discovered that he had been in a course in British History for about six weeks, when he should have been in a course in American History. So we rounded him up and talked to him and asked him how that happened? Why did he not recognize the fact that he was somewhere in the wrong place? He said, "I kept wondering when the professor was going to start talking about the United States and stop talking so much about England." Finally, we got him relocated--really we should have thrown him out. He stood there towering over me, then he reached down and grabbed my shoulder just like he would handle a basketball and said, "Kid, I'm awful sorry I forgot about you."

He didn't last very long as an academician or a basketball player.

B. C.: What problem, if any, did the academic interest of the University of Kentucky, more especially the faculty, have in competing for attention in resources with athletic interests during the Rupp years?

T.C.: The so-called Rupp years came at a period in the history of the university from 1930 down to the time that

Adolph Rupp retired. I believe that was in 1969 or 1970--I'm not sure about the date. In that time, a great many changes occurred. Not only changes, but many incidents took place which resulted in the state of and bearing on the athletic program and the general morale of the university itself. Down until World War II, the faculty didn't feel as far away from the athletic program as it did after that time. It didn't feel the great pressure that developed in the Southeastern Conference, for instance. But I must say that a more sensible answer is that the academic world lived pretty far apart from the athletic world. The two had altogether different objectives. The academic world strove to improve the conditions of the intellectual undertakings, the intellectual objectives of the university. The athletic world strove to improve the university's success and image in the field of athletics. Those two things could hardly ever meet.

Nevertheless, in the early years, the athletic coaches were very much involved in the academic community. They attended the university general faculty entertainments, they developed friendships among the professorial staff--in fact, they, along with the faculty, constituted one academic family.

Adolph Rupp came to the university a bright young man from the University of Kansas, where he had been a student under the great Coach Phog Allen of that institution. He also had taken classes under Professor Frank Hodder, who had a reputation--some considerable reputation--in the field of American history. Rupp had a keen interest in history. He came to our offices at Frazee Hall on many occasions and sat down and talked about what was going on in the academic field. I am sure he had in the back of his mind the intention of doing graduate work and maybe going into the field of teaching history if the athletic business didn't pay off for him. Rupp, as you know, came into a southern conference where basketball was not the primary sport. The old southern conference schools had devoted their attentions largely to baseball and football, in neither of which Kentucky had been unusually successful. As a matter of fact, baseball and football I think might be considered secondary to basketball. As Rupp advanced in his years of coaching, he became more and more successful, attracting more attention, both in the region and in the nation. Of course, winning the national championship four times, added greatly to his stature as a coach. I don't remember ever hearing a faculty member--that is a purely academic faculty member--ever say anything that indicated any jealousy of one sort or another toward the Rupp basketball program. I did know that there was a great deal of jealousy between the basketball coach and the football coaches. The history of the university in the area of football was one of making changes quite frequently of head football coaches. And it was said that came about largely because of jealousy between Rupp and the football coaches and because of a great emphasis on basketball.

Kentucky, in its whole educational history, affects some of the conditions which have led to some of the development of such an avid interest in basketball. Earlier, a lack of funds in the largely rural high schools across the state, meant only a limited number of high schools could organize and maintain football teams--partly for lack of financial support, and partly for lack of sufficient players to fill a highly competitive team. One thing the schools could do, no matter where they were located, whether it be high up in a mountain county or in one of the towns or cities in other parts of the state, the schools could mount a good basketball team, and basketball became the primary sport in the Commonwealth. And when Rupp came on the scene, he found little difficulty in recruiting good basketball players.

I'd like to say in this connection--in the early years, Rupp was a very strict disciplinarian so far as his players were concerned. He saw to it that they got down and did their class work. When you had one of Rupp's students in your class, you were pretty well assured that he was going to do creditable work. As a matter of fact, some of the basketball players of the early period did more than creditable work--they did very exemplary work and they succeeded in life after they left the university.

Just before World War II began, the university began to ease its way into the high pressure, almost professional area of basketball players. World War II pretty well stripped the university of basketball playing talent. However, they did field a team, I believe, all four years. They had a team that, relatively speaking and comparatively speaking, was a highly successful venture. After World War II, athletics at the university entered into a new phase. There was a great pressure at the institution in both the areas of basketball and football to build winning teams. Basketball had already established itself, and football was rapidly coming up in the world.

Around the 1950's there was tremendous pressure--tremendous excitement and emphasis on athletics, especially on basketball. There occurred in the late 1940's and early 50's, the basketball scandal which came out of boys fixing games, betting on the outcome of games, which resulted in a very unsettling and embarrassing situation for the University of Kentucky. A new athletic board was formed and on the face of things, new approaches were made to athletic management. I'm not so sure that very much was accomplished in that area.

In the years of the 1950's, Rupp had become a major figure on the campus. I doubt very seriously that any other person, including the president of the university, enjoyed so much name recognition and so much public popularity as did Adolph Rupp. I know in those days when the Alumni Association would gather alumni in meetings over the state, nearly always they would request that the university would send up somebody who could talk about athletics. I was impressed, and still am, with the fact that the academic aspect of the university in their minds was put in a secondary position.

By that time, athletics had become almost completely separated from the academic program, so that the faculty went its way doing its best to build as successful an academic program as the university had developed athletic programs. That was an uphill battle. From 1930 to 1968--the years I was connected with the university--there was an eternal struggle to get from the state legislature and other sources of support enough money to keep the university operating with some margin of support for an improvement of the academic program. If as much emphasis, as much public interest, had been demonstrated on behalf of the academic program as was demonstrated for the athletic program, the university could have gained twice the ground over those years as it did. I used to go to the games and see that great mass of people who sat there yelling their heads off and I wondered how many of them really knew, or cared as far as that was concerned, much about the academic program of the university. I was tempted on many occasions to ask one of those rabid, yelling fans how much he knew about the university and its academic endeavors? I doubt that he knew very much. A lot of times that loud-mouthed fan was not a graduate of the university and possibly had never been inside the institution as an academic registrant.

The faculty had tremendous challenges to try to build a sound academic program in both the graduate and undergraduate fields. It was a rugged uphill fight to build a good library and maintain laboratories and to venture into the rapidly developing new fields that began to make heavy demands on our American academic community after World War II. As far as I was concerned, athletics in that latter period had become seriously over emphasized. I am still of the opinion that far too much emphasis was placed on intercollegiate athletics. Institutions can't help but get in trouble. The alumni and the public place a tremendous pressure on institutions to win games. Winning seems to be the main objective, not the development of a successful competitive program in a sane collegiate way.

I had an experience that convinced me how far, really, the public attitude toward athletics had gone. I served on a search committee seeking a new president, after the retirement of president Frank Dickey. On that committe were members of the faculty and members of the Board of Trustees. Sometimes I was embarrassed when we brought prospective candidates to the campus, when a member of the Board of Trustees asked their first question of the candidate, how he felt about intercollegiate athletics. I felt that should have been nearer the foot of the list of questions that should be asked of a man who was being interviewed for the purpose of determining who could provide the best leadership in developing a first-class, highly mature academic program.

Back to Rupp. I knew Adolph personally. We came here at practically the same time. I saw him on many occasions and talked with him several times. Personally, I liked him very much. He had a very attractive personality. There was no doubt--not the slightest doubt in my mind that he was a genius. Not only was he a genius in coaching basketball, he was shrewd in the area of public relations. I have never known a man who did a better job of selling himself to the public than Adolph did. Adolph was a man of singlemindedness. He knew his own strengths and he practiced them with intensity. He was a successful writer. Adolph had an impressive personality. He had a keen sense of humor and at the same time he could be pretty obstreperous on occasions when he thought that his interest was being threatened.

I would recommend a much more intelligent and much fuller appraisal of Rupp, the reading of Bert Nelli's book, *Basketball at the University of Kentucky.* I think through that book you get glimpses, in fact you get a good analysis of the impact of Adolph Rupp, not only on the sport of basketball and upon the Southeastern Conference, but upon Kentucky and the University of Kentucky.

B. C.: Who are some of the more interesting people you have known over the years?

T. C.: Over the years since 1928, when I first came to Kentucky, I have met many unusual men and women. In picking out unsung Kentuckians or famous Kentuckians--it's very difficult to single out just a few of the unusual people I have known.

I think Urey Woodson, who once was editor of the *Owensboro Messenger*, and later was very active in the national affairs of the Democratic Party was a tremendously exciting person. I felt after knowing him, and I had a great deal of correspondence with him and I knew him personally, that I literally turned backwards into the nineteenth century and came on into the first decades of this century with a very capable guide--a man who knew the ins and outs of Kentucky politics. He knew the personalities--their virtues and their shortcomings--he knew about the ambitions of politicians, and those of businessmen, lobbyists and all of the political shenanigans that occurred before, during, and after the Goebel affair. He knew intimately the ins and outs of the national Democratic Party affairs, and that is to say that he knew a great deal of the operation and manipulation of politics by both the Democratic and Republican parties on the national scene. He knew personalities in the national field and was able to bring them down to grassroots level and present them as human beings, as personalities with all the problems, all the personal traits and all the weaknesses and natures of humans in general.

I especially enjoyed my conversations with him about the Goebel affair. He campaigned for Goebel, knew inside and out of what went on in that campaign. He was able to refute countless stories about the Goebel campaign and the Goebel affair. I remember him saying that Goebel began his campaign in Bowling Green, and for some reason, he fainted and fell on the platform and there fell out of his pocket a dirk knife. Goebel's supporters were horrified. If that got out in the newspapers and to the public generally, there would have been great harm. Whoever picked up the knife quickly pushed it back in Goebel's pocket and said, "It's only a large comb." And he got out of that embarrassing situation with a certain amount of grace. Woodson also told me they had worked very hard to get Goebel and William Jennings Bryan together. Woodson had worked out an agreement between them as to their philosophies and relations in that period of progressive agrarian unrest. They were in St. Louis, I suppose at a political rally. And Goebel agreed to meet with Bryan and Bryan agreed to meet with Goebel. They took Bryan up to Goebel's hotel room and Goebel was on the commode. He greeted Bryan in that situation and that insulted him. They were never able to get the two together again.

I could not pass over knowing A. O. Stanley. There must be a million stories about Stanley as Governor and as

Senator, and later as Commissioner of the International Boundary. As I have said earlier, he was as full of stories as any man I have ever known. Most of them had to do with his relationship with Ed Morrow. They were rivals who campaigned, I think as I said earlier, sleeping in the same bed, in the same hotel room, riding side by side on mules, and then jerking the hide off of each other on the stump. They remained very close friends throughout the rest of their lives. I never did know Governor Morrow--if I ever saw him, I don't recall.

There was William H. Townsend. I got to know Bill Townsend when I came back to Kentucky in 1930, I believe it was in the summer of 1930, to do some special work in the bibliographical field. We remained intimate friends down until the time of his death. He was one of the most attractive story tellers that I have ever known. He was simply a genius at telling stories. He had the memory of an elephant and the talent for adding color to even the most commonplace thing. I heard Bill Townsend's stories over and over and they never ceased to be interesting to me, because I always wanted to know what new twist he would give to them.

I could say that there are many other Kentuckians that I would have liked to have known. I would have liked to have known George D. Prentice, founder of the *Louisville Journal,* who became one of the most colorful of the American newspaper editors. From 1830 down to 1868, Prentice was an editorial voice that was heard all across the nation. He was a personality that was unpredictable, really, but never dull--always ready with an apt, sometimes very acid, response to situations.

I would have liked to have known Harriette Arnow. I have enormous respect for her as an author. I think she will be regarded as one of Kentucky's most solid authors. I think she will not occupy the high place that Robert Penn Warren occupies, but she will be right up there close behind him.

By the way, I have known Robert Penn Warren over the years, and in my casual association with him, I have enjoyed knowing him indeed. He is a very impressive man. He is a very human, friendly, down-to-earth individual. And above all, he is a genius. He is one of Kentucky's most distinguished citizens of all times. And certainly he is at the top of Kentucky's author list. Barry Bingham of the Louisville *Courier Journal* has been for me an enormously interesting personality. I think Barry has been one of the most constructive, progressive, and farsighted Kentuckians of all times. His paper, the *Courier Journal*, certainly has an enormous impact on the affairs in the Commonwealth of Kentucky.

One could go on enlarging upon this list of interesting individuals--John Sherman Cooper was a tremendously fascinating personality. A. B. Chandler is a personality that will not be forgotten in this state--maybe ever. He will go down in history as a landmark personality. Senator Alben W. Barkley, I think, will enjoy a rather long historical life in this state.

I could go on reciting many other persons, but these are enough to give you an insight into some of the Kentuckians who were around when I came here and during the time that I was a professor in the university, and some of the Kentuckians who lived in the past.

For instance, wouldn't it have been interesting to sit down and talk with Jane Todd Crawford about her experiences in that famous operation that Dr. Ethan McDowell performed in the removal of that ovarian tumor? I think maybe that would have made a book within itself. So would a conversation with Dr. McDowell.

B. C.: Who are some of the more well known national personalities you have encountered?

T. C.: Well, earlier, as I said, I met Charles Curtis who became the Vice-President on the Hoover ticket during the election of 1928. He was the first Republican I ever saw who was not a postmaster.

I have known Robert Penn Warren.

I served on the Truman Library Board with Earl Warren, Chief Justice of the United States Supreme Court. On two or three occasions, he and I walked along and talked about affairs. I asked him on one of those occasions if he had it all to do over, would he make any different decision in *Brown* vs. *School Board of Education*. He said emphatically that he would not change that decision in any way. He knew that it was going to stand; he knew that decision was going to create enormous commotion in the country, a great emotional upheaval--which it did. But in the long run, it would bring revolutionary changes in the racial and social relationships of the nation.

I have known several publishers, Lawrence Chambers of the Bobbs Merrill Company; John Farrar of the Farrar-Rinehart Company--I knew very well Alfred Knopf of the Alfred Knopf Publishing House.

I would not take anything for my association with Herman B. Wells, the famous president of Indiana University. During my six years on that staff, Chancellor Wells and I became very good friends and I cherish that friendship.

I also developed a friendship with Mr. Eli Lily, of the famous Eli Lily Company. Mr. Lily was the grandson of the founder of that business--an exceedingly interesting man and a very human individual. My wife and I were their house guests and I saw him on many occasions when I was in Indiana.

I came to know very casually Clark Kerr of the University of California. I knew him after he had left that university.

I have known many historians that have made national reputations. As a matter of fact, I came on in a generation of historians when you were still able to meet the older generation--the founding fathers. I have lived through about four generations of historians, and there were many distinguished scholars among them.

I have known many other individuals that reached national prominence--John Sherman Cooper, for instance, was a man that I respected and still respect enormously. He was a man who served this state well as Senator. He served this country exceedingly well as Ambassador to India. He has been a very staunch individual in representing Kentucky on many occasions and in many challenges.

I was in India with Chester Bowles, who was also a

famous ambassador. I had an enormous respect for him.

B. C.: Are there any unsung or unheralded Kentuckians whom you think deserve more credit than they have received?

T. C.: So many times you are asked to single out famous Kentuckians. I almost view this as being an act of futility. Who can stand up here and act like God and look through three million people and see among them certain individuals who stand out far above the crowd, or find in those three million people--those highly deserving, self-effacing, long-suffering, unsung heroes? That is just impossible to do. If you attempt to do it, you are certain to do injustice--gross injustice--to some deserving individuals, and I'm not about to get into that business of hurting anyone, because there are literally hundreds and thousands of Kentuckians who, in their own way and with their keen abilities and devotions and determination, have served this Commonwealth loyally and well.

I am, however, going to single out one group that must be listed as Kentucky's great heroes. Whatever their shortcomings as individuals may be, whatever their shortcomings as collective groups may be, those things do not detract from the fact that the men and women who have served this Commonwealth as teachers in the elementary schools, high schools, special high schools, junior colleges, and universities are unsung Kentuckians. That, of course, is not true of individuals--individual teachers in local communities, individuals in larger academic organizations that have been recognized. But where one person has been recognized, a dozen more just as deserving have been overlooked. Collectively, over the long range of history, the teacher has been Bruce at the bridge, trying to drag this Commonwealth out of a state of inadequate, educational efforts into the realm of high standards of educational excellence. I listen to all of the criticism of teachers, and certainly I think much of it might be deserved. They are inadequately trained in many cases, they are incapable in many individual cases. Some are lazy, they are self-serving, possibly. They have all the faults of other human beings and of every other collective professional group which has a name. There are, however, enough individuals within the collective body to give solid substance and genuine dignity and lasting meaning to the accomplishments of their profession. I have no objection to the testing of teachers. It seems to me that all the talk is on the matter of testing, trying to make sure that there are adequate teachers in the classroom. That certainly is an admirable objective. But, at the same time, I have yet to hear an adequate discussion of the positive services rendered by the teaching profession in Kentucky and the collective educational bodies. Teachers must hear and heed the current discussions of their profession, but the public must respect the teachers as a most important key functionary in our society.

B. C.: Why, in your opinion, are Kentucky people so reluctant to approve changes in our state constitution?

T. C.: I have a notion--I don't know whether you could sustain this with all the facts or not. The years of 1880 and 1890 were years in which people became very frightened in this state of forces--politicians, corporations, the oil brigadiers who were in control of public affairs--and when the delegates came into the Constitutional Convention of 1890 and 1891, they wanted to stabilize everything. And I can see why, in the context of that moment, that would be true. They wanted to stabilize their lives and the affairs of the Commonwealth. They drafted a regulatory constitution, which became a mill stone about this state's neck. The people so far have refused to change it.

Then came along the Goebel campaign, and the Goebel assassination, that created an enormous amount of anger against the corporations and the corporations created an enormous amount of fear. When Goebel was killed, the state was so shocked about all of that, and it struck so fundamentally at law and order, that the people became more reluctant than ever to accept change. The state was involved in the feuds in the mountains and in the Black Patch War in western Kentucky and in all kinds of social chaos throughout the state. The government became almost too paralyzed to act, and that inherent tear has carried on working its influence in a big way in this state, even today.

We have been reluctant to accept any change of the constitution and its administrative form of government. The changes that have come have virtually been forced on us. For instance, the county jails are in such miserable condition that the federal and state inspectors have condemned the jails in some of our counties. So jailors have had to rush around and find another county with a jail where they will house their prisoners. In Estill County, for instance, that jailor loaded up his prisoners and took them down to Frankfort, and got a terrific scolding from the attorney general.

B. C.: So the new constitution of 1890, which Goebel helped write, was a highly regulatory document?

T. C.: Yes. As I said before, 1890 was a moment of great agitation, a moment of bitter antagonism between the corporate control of this state and the populist control.

It was necessary, the delegates thought, to stabilize the state for a long time to come. Well, they couldn't see what fundamental changes were coming in American society and in American political organization. The General Assembly has spent the time since 1890 trying to do two things--trying to amend the constitution and trying to really get it revised in a wholescale manner. It has also bypassed it in a lot of respects.

B. C.: So you think the bloody Goebel affair which immediately followed the writing of that constitution put people in such a state of mind as to have been resistant to change ever since?

T. C.: I have a notion that the shock of those affairs had a very definite bearing on our reaction to government.

B. C.: You were born in 1903 and you've plowed behind a mule, talked to the soldiers of Lee and Forrest, flown around the world, and watched men walk on the moon. Do you think that we've seen more social and cultural changes in this century than any other century in the annals of mankind?

T. C.: Oh, yes. There is not any doubt about that. We see in every decade more changes than occurred in one quarter or half-century in the past.

As for far-reaching revolutionary changes, look what's happened in the field of electronics. Every Tom, Dick and Harry is running around chattering about computers. Every sort of information is on computers. You buy something in a store and it has that electronic computer label on it, and they run it by a sensor and take information off of that. You go to some libraries to borrow a book and there is no longer a card catalog--there is a computer terminal that locates a book and does whatever you want it to do. You could just go on and on. In the field of medicine, there are people who will be living ten years from now who thirty years ago might not have been alive because we might not have had the medical knowledge that is here now to keep us alive. Longevity is becoming a real issue in our society--in both Kentucky and American society. Oh sure, there have been phenomenal changes, and if the prognosticators are right, we are just on the edge of a real breakthrough on so many things. Undoubtedly, we will come up with answers to many matters. We have already come up with some and I suppose some of them are amazing answers to that infernal curse of human beings--cancer. We have learned a lot more about the disease but we have not learned how to combat it. That goes with all kinds of diseases. Pneumonia is no longer the dreaded disease it once was. Arthritis...maybe somebody will find something to treat that.

B. C.: Do you believe that the changes of the next century will be as rapid and shocking as the changes of this century?

T. C.: I simply do not know the answer to that. Maybe so.

We have not invented everything--we have not come to the end of that road. The more you introduce, the more you invent and the more changes you bring about in the structure of society. That is where the revolutionary revelations are going to come--how these things change structures of society, change the approach we have to problems.

B. C.: What would be your preferred future for Kentucky?

T. C.: One in which it is educating its precious human resource to take a creative, productive place without the humiliation of being classified as low on the statistical scale, or low on other meaningful tables of measurement. One in which we are living in communities that are decentralized as much as possible and as free of social maladjustments as is possible for a community to be. By that I mean of crime, of poverty, of social failure in general, and free of the divisive elements which creep into a diseased society. I would want to see Kentucky control its precious human resource. You are not going to displace the human being completely with robotics and other labor saving devices.

B. C.: What major areas of human endeavors do you anticipate that Kentucky will be noted for 100 years from now?

T. C.: I cannot even begin to visualize an answer to that question.

B. C.: In what area do you think that Kentucky can step up and take a unique place compared with other states which would attract people to come here either to go to school or to live or that would give recognition to Kentucky as being in the vanguard of a particular social field?

T. C.: I know of nothing that would improve conditions in Kentucky and give it future status more than a highly effective, efficient educational system. Beyond that, it is hard for me to see how anything else could thrive in the state. For me, just sitting here in these onrushing days of that approaching twenty-first century, and try to say what it will be at the close of the next would be pretty stupid. If you just simply tried to translate in terms of the individual, what kind of house he will live in, what kind of food he will be eating, what kind of services he will be demanding, what employment he will have--that is hard to do. Nobody in 1900 could have predicted that Kentucky would have the modern highway system that it now has. One could not have visualized the great body of statutory law that pertains to the revolutionary changes that have taken place in Kentucky society since 1900, or have visualized the state of medicine of 1999. That is a field where you could run wild with speculation.

I do not think there is going to be this free and easy rural Kentuckian in the twenty-first century. Kentuckians are going to be lucky if they are to function as individuals in future society. I raise a question in my mind about something. They are getting ready to add the two-millionth book to the University of Kentucky Library. That raises the question--in the next century, what is going to be the fate of the book? Are we still going to be producing books? Are people still going to be taking in the knowledge of things, the concept of the past, the concept of things about them by reading? Or are they going to be wholly influenced by audio-visual and computerized processes?

B. C.: What do you think about that?

T. C.: Of course, I do not know the answers. My notion is that there is going to be more and more audio-visual perception than perception by extensive reading and the extensive use of books. I think we will go on producing books--I believe and hope we will--but I think books will come to have a different impact on society.

B. C.: But aren't there more books published today, even in the wake of more audio-visual techniques than at any other time?

T. C.: Yes, and to a certain extent the audio-visual techniques stimulate interest in books. I think that has to be said. You mention favorably a book on television on a "Today" show interview, for instance. That sells thousands of copies. Or the mention of it on national television in any way results in a tremendous response.

B. C.: Would you equate the changes of today in Kentucky with the intensity of the changes which occurred immediately after the Civil War?

T. C.: Yes. Obviously, no two periods of history ever come down in the same way. That was a period of redirection. You are right in that assumption. It was a period of political, social, and industrial upheaval. It was a period of fresh beginnings--in education, in the building of railroads, in bringing into the state certain industries, in the introduction of a new crop. Burley tobacco came into prominence in this era. The competitiveness of the rail system had developed.

The current period, however, is one that is not going to be based so much on just the old-fashioned labor--human energy, strong human backs--but upon the sophisticated, technological phase of production. We are entering an age, as I understand it from everything I read, which indicates service employment in all of the electronics, of the specialized services which will be rendered to society, will be the basic thing, and not only the state economy but also in the national and international economy. That, of course, is putting an entirely different shoe on the foot than you were dealing with in the period right after the Civil War. For instance, I think the challenges and the meeting of those challenges of the post Civil War period were more comprehensible than are the challenges of the moment. I think one of the problems for the large mass of Kentuckians is the incomprehensibility of what is coming. What will be the shape of the twenty-first century, where does the individual come down in this highly changing, highly complex service society that we are going to have? You see the handwriting on the wall in the future of the automated automobile industry, for instance. Who would have ever thought that the American automobile industry would be so severely shaken by outside competition? Who would have ever thought that the iron and steel industry would be so severely impacted by outside influence? Who would have ever thought that the great textile industry would be so severely handicapped by outside competition--and so it goes. We, as a national people, still have frontiers if we can realize them, and that will be in the technological-electronics-scientific services fields.

B. C.: Henry Watterson was the man with the Courier-Journal who shaped or helped to shape our thinking during that transition state after the Civil War. Do you anticipate that a like personality or a like member of the media will have that type of an impact during this time?

T. C.: I think the day of the old personal editor is gone. The editorial pages of the newpaper to me are largely collaborative affairs of editorial staffs with too little of a discernible personal touch day-after-day-after-day.

Historically, Kentuckians have cherished the state's rich tradition of personal journalism. The radio and television have changed this. I would imagine that an increasingly large proportion of the state's population depend on television for news, information, and recreation.

B. C.: Do you forsee that there is a real danger that we will destroy our natural resources and the environment to the point that Kentucky will lose its personality and character for natural beauty and bountiful resources?

T. C.: We are acting like drunken sailors in the management of our resources.

Let's take the first example. One of the most precious resources we have is the most common one we have--water. Look how we have polluted our streams. We have desecrated our streams as though a pure water supply is of no consequence. I do not know about the Green and Barren rivers, or the Tennessee and the lower Cumberland. They are big streams, especially when you get into the impoundment areas. But you go into Eastern Kentucky into the Kentucky River system and you see debris and solid waste of every sort imaginable that human beings can throw into water. Much of the water Kentuckians drink is said to bear a heavy burden of chemical contamination. Plus, there's another disturbing evil sign--siltation. The silting of the streams from strip mines or land erosion is going to be an enormously costly fact in this state's future. Kentucky has an abundance of water, but we are being wasteful, we are careless and neglectful of our water resources. We are living in an age where we are going to have to pay very strict attention to the conservation of this precious resource.

You almost talk to deaf ears in Kentucky about a second commonplace resource, one that we have taken so much for granted that we have done deep injury to it. That is the forest resource. Kentucky once was a wilderness state. Our whole frontier heritage and legend centers around the forest. We have cut the virgin forest out and have raped the second growth woods over and over. The state forestry department and other agencies have struggled to renew this precious resource. We have light miles to go to reclaim and put on the road to professional production this highly precious and renewable resource.

Our very land is another resource. We really are not in a position right now, in my opinion, to draw any firm conclusions as to whether strip-mined land can really be made productive again. If so, how productive? Productive of what? Quality timber? These are still questions for which the answers are not now available. Yet we are stripping land every day in areas of Kentucky. The surface is being laid bare, the dirt is washing down, soil is being carried away, streams are being choked, water resources are being contaminated with chemicals, and so you go.

There is a blessed thing about the Appalachian Kentucky, and it is true of the Pennyrile and western Kentucky--in all that general area that is called western Kentucky--the forests are renewable, and quickly renewable. The Appalachians for instance, if left alone will restore timber cover rather quickly. It will not always restore itself with the most desirable timber, that is true, but it has a very high recovery capability.

As to the beauty of this state--you drive along and see trash that people dump on the roadside where the counties are too poor to maintain garbage and solid waste collections and establish landfills. You come upon nauseating dump sites where people pull up along the side of the road and throw out everything in creation, just pile the stuff up. When you see that in a community, you see one that has not a chance in the world of getting an industry of any sophistication to locate. You will see the badge of a community that lacks pride, lacks an appreciation of what appearance and these very simple things mean in the long range of economic and social advancement.

B. C.: How would you like to see Kentucky celebrate its bicentennial in 1992?

T. C.: If I am around in 1992, which I don't think I will be--it would be in a wheelchair--if I have a clear mind, which maybe I've never had, and if I have any voice that I can lift, I would wish that Kentucky would celebrate not only the 200 years existence of the Commonwealth and the development of a unified people, but I would like to see it celebrate its 200th anniversary by drafting a new constitution. One which would prepare the Commonwealth for the twenty-first century with a modern, progressive government in keeping with what the prophets say will be the challenges of the next century. I certainly am not advocating any radical drafting of any far out document. What I am advocating is an outright, honest, forthright change.

Within the past 100 years enormous changes have taken place in Kentucky, tremendous modernizations have occurred in the area of government, economic endeavors, in the sociological areas, in the educational areas. All human endeavors in Kentucky have undergone fundamental changes and the challenges will be brand new. They are not those of 1892. They are the challenges of 1992, and more important than that, they will be the challenges of the new twenty-first century. Why should Kentucky handicap itself by stumbling into the next century with a fundamental governmental document that is not adequate enough to allow the state to meet those challenges? It seems to me that at no time in the history of the state that we have had more talent, more capabilities, and more forthright perspective on the part of people and prospective delegates, to draw up a modern constitution that will protect all the rights of all Kentuckians, that will protect every institution that we hold near and dear. At the same time we need to do for Kentucky what a complete revision of a modern corporation would do for its reorganization and modernization. Kentucky could bring itself into the new century with more than a grand promise to modernize its government in the constitutional area.

I am reminded when A. B. Chandler became governor in the 1930's, one of the first acts was to reorganize state government. And those who have read that reorganization act realize that what he did was drag Kentucky literally out of the first half of the nineteenth century and bring it into the fourth decade of the twentieth century--that's exactly what I am talking about in the reorganization of the Kentucky constitution itself.

I think one other thing that I would hope for Kentucky in the new century, is with all the displacements--economic and sociological--of this state which have been taking place since World War II, that some element of a solid agrarian way of life could be preserved. I would hope that we will not rush into a new century leaving behind all of the cherished institutions of the past, because there are many solid human values, many cherished institutional values in the agrarian history of Kentucky.

First and foremost of anything I could wish for this, my adopted state, would be the creation of sane policies regarding Kentucky's precious human and natural resources. A glorious way to open a new century would be to make sure that every individual capable of taking educational training would have an opportunity to become adequately prepared to make periodic adaptations to changing times. A horrible way to begin a new era would be to allow more than a million Kentuckians to remain non-competitive in the new technological age because of functional illiteracy. Above all I would hope that the Commonwealth would not tolerate the development of a congenital welfare class incapable of becoming productive citizens. Education of increasing efficiency must be the answer.

A central theme of Kentucky history has been its land and natural resources. These have not belonged to any single generation. Future Kentuckians have as much claim on the land and the natural resouces as had the pioneers who first entered the western country. To destroy the land by unregulated mining practices, by allowing erosion to take place, by stream pollution, and the contamination of the fresh water resource would be sinful. This same thing applies to Kentucky's timber resource. One must hope that the younger generation of Kentuckians will become resource conscious, protecting the land, the streams, and the woods. These have been, and will continue to be, foundation stones of Kentucky civilization.

"So Kentucky's worlds revolve perpetually in concentric, Saturn-like circles, which, whirling around each other without merging, glory in the fact that they are part of the Commonwealth. Physically, modern Kentucky is at once a land of breath-taking natural beauty and a testimonial to man's defilement. The haze-shrouded folds of hills which roll out from Pine Mountain are soul-lifting in majesty and space. This pastoral Kentucky, however, is rapidly being submerged by the invasion of industry, crowded shopping malls, urban sprawl, and a rapidly growing non-farm population. What was once a great wilderness Eden is now laced together by million-dollar-a-mile highways which slash through rocky hillsides and thrust across rivers to collapse distances and erase sectional boundaries. A modern traveler can traverse Daniel Boone's two-year journey in less than two hours and not break the fifty-five-mile speed limit.

The longhunters, trailbreakers, and land scouts themselves planted the seeds of change. For two centuries their descendants nurtured those seeds. They have dammed up rivers to create vast lakes, gnawed their way through mountains to snatch up rich veins of coal and strewn the countrysides with the artifacts of modern civilization. Yet blessed islands of nature remain in the Daniel Boone National Forest, the national monuments about Cumberland Gap, Mammoth Cave, and the Lincoln Homestead, and in the wilderness peninsula between the Cumberland and Tennessee rivers. Not always astute in protecting its rich natural resources, Kentucky does preserve the sites of the Natural Bridge, Cumberland Falls, Carter Caves, Lilly's Woods, and a half dozen other historic and natural areas. And Louisville distiller, Isaac Bernheim, dedicated his Muldraugh Hills knob land holdings as a magnificent public preserve.

If it were possible to stay the changes that the passage of time brings, most Kentuckians would choose to maintain the status quo. Self-assured prophets are certain that at the end of this century, Kentucky's foundation stone--the subsistence family farm--will be a museum place; that the population will almost have doubled; that in place of man's traditional relationships with the land an urban society will claw furiously at the hills to create standing room. These prophets ignore the historic fact that after two centuries Kentucky still holds green breathing space.

Kentucky's rural traditions took shape in that time of leisurely seasoning, and there still thrives a vibrant group of obstinate and provincial humanity in the broad stretch of territory between Cumberland Gap and Reelfoot Lake who are ready if necessary to stand off a radical thrust of change, even the sudden burst of the revolutionary, twenty-first century."

THOMAS D. CLARK

Born: July 14, 1903, Louisville, Mississippi.

Educated:

Common Schools Winston County, Mississippi.
Choctaw Agricultural High School, 1921-1925, graduate April 1925.
University of Mississippi, 1925-1928, A.B. degree 1929.
Attended University of Virginia, 1928.
University of Kentucky, September 1928, M.A. degree in 1929.
Duke University, September 1929, Ph.D. degree 1932.

Experience:

Instructor, Memphis State College, 1930.
University of Tennessee, 1931.
Instructor, University of Kentucky, 1931.
Assistant Professor, 1936-1939; Associate Professor, 1939-1942.
Professor, 1942-1950.
Distinguished Professor, 1950-1968.
Head of the Department of History, 1942-1965.
Sesquicentennial Professor, Indiana University, 1966-1967.
Distinguished Service Professor, 1968-1973.
Distinguished Professor, Eastern Kentucky University, 1973-1976.
Bingham Professor, University of Louisville, 1974.

Visiting Professor:

University of Rochester
Duke University
University of North Carolina
University of Chicago
Harvard University
University of Wisconsin
Pennsylvania State University
Claremont Graduate School
Briefly research staff Vanderbilt University
University of Wyoming
University of Washington
Stanford University

Foreign Assignments:

Salzburg Seminar, 1948
Professor, University of Vienna, 1949-1950
Foreign Service U.S. State Department in India, 1952
Lecturer, American Seminar in Oxford University
Lecturer, American-Yugo Slav Seminar
NATO Professor, University of Athens and Thessalonica in Greece

Professional Assignments:

President of the Southern Historical Association and chairman of various committees--including the planning committee which redirected the efforts of the Association.
Editor, Journal of Southern History, 1948-1952.
President, Mississippi Valley Historical Association (Now the Organization of American Historical Association.) Chairman of its Executive Committee for six years. Chairman of its planning and revisionary committee which resulted in the changing of the names of the Review to the Journal of American History.
Served as the Executive Secretary of the OAH from 1970-1973 for the purpose of organizing the national headquarters in Indiana University.
President, Phi Alpha Theta honorary history fraternity.
Member of several of the committees of the American Historical Association.
Board of Directors of the Kentucky Historical Society.
Member of the Kentucky Archives Commission, serving as its first chairman.
Chairman of the University of Kentucky Press Committee, and effected the organization of the University Press of Kentucky.
Chairman of the Committee of Fifteen entrusted with the responsibility of reorganizing the University of Kentucky's academic program.
Member of the Board of Trustees of the University of Kentucky.

Non Academic Offices:

Member Board of Trustees of Henry Clay Memorial Foundation.
Trustee of Pleasant Hill at Shakertown in Kentucky.

Author:

Beginning of the L & N, 1933

A Pioneer Southern Railroad, Cairo to New Orleans, (University of North Carolina Press), 1936

A History of Kentucky, (Prentice-Hall), 1937

The Kentucky, (Rivers of America Series, Farrar and Rinehart), 1941

The Rampaging Frontier, (Bobbs-Merrill), 1939

Pills, Petticoats and Plows, (Bobbs-Merrill), 1944

The Southern Country Editor, (Bobbs-Merrill), 1948

The Rural Editor and the New South, (Louisiana Press), 1948

Bluegrass Cavalcade, (University of Kentucky Press), 1962

Frontier America, (Scribners), 1957

The Emerging South, (Oxford), 1961

The South Since Appamattox (With A. D. Kirwan), (Oxford), 1964

Three Paths to the Modern South, (University of Georgia Press), 1965

Indiana University, Midwest Pioneer, 4 vols., (Indiana University Press), 1970-1976

Historic Maps of Kentucky, (Univ. Press of Kentucky), 1979

Kentucky, Land of Contrast, (Harper & Rowe), 1969

The Greening of the South, (University Press of Kentucky), 1984

A Century of Banking in the Bluegrass, (The John Bradford Press), 1982

Books Edited:

William Littell, *Festoons of Fancy*, University of Kentucky Press, (Won the Graphic Arts Award).

Harry Toulmin, *Descriptions of Kentucky*, University of Kentucky Press, (Made the Rockefeller Graphic Arts Tour).

John MaGill, *The Kentuckian to the Emigrant*, University Kentucky Press, (Unanimous choice of the Graphic Arts Jury).

Elisha D. Perkins, *Gold Rush Diary*, University of Kentucky Press, 1967.

Travels in the Old South (3 vols), University of Oklahoma Press, 1956, 1959.

Travels in the Confederacy, Oklahoma, 1948.

Travels in the New South (2 vols), University of Oklahoma Press, 1962.

Charles Glass Gray, *Off at Sunrise (Gold Rush Diary)*, Huntington Library Press, 1976.

South Carolina, the Grand Tour, University of South Carolina Press, 1971.

The South Since Reconstruction, Bobbs-Merrill, 1973.

The Great American Frontier, Bobbs-Merrill.

Edwin Bryant, *What I Saw in California*, University of Nebraska Press, 1985.

Clark has contributed chapters to several collaborative works, and to most of the encyclopedias, plus the regional ones. He has published numerous articles in professional journals.

Phi Theta Kappa (Duke Chapter).
Guggenheim Fellowship.
Member American Council of the Humanities (secretaries section) , 1973.
Member Board of the Truman Library, 1970-1973.

Lectures:

The Lilly Lectures, Wabash College.
The Fleming Lectures, Louisiana State University.
The Lamar Memorial Lectures, Mercer University.
Phi Beta Kappa Lecturer.

Awards:

Distinguished Alumni Award, University of Mississippi, 1979.
Kentucky Alumni Hall of Fame.
University of Kentucky Teaching Award, 1968.
University of Kentucky Research Award, 1968.
Distinguished Citizenship Award, Governor's Medal, Commonwealth of Kentucky.
Gold Medal Good Citizenship Award, Sons of the American Revolution.
Tom Wallace Forestry Award, 1961.
Forestry Recognition Award, 1963, Kentucky-Tennessee Section.
Society of American Foresters.
Distinguished Service Award, Kiwanis Club, 1982.
Kentucky Media Award, 1983-1984.
Kentucky Oral History Award, 1981.
Distinguished Service Recognition, Organization of American Historians, 1984.
National Endowment for the Humanities Citation for organization of the National Newspaper Conservation and Directory Project, 1983.

Honorary Degrees:

Indiana University
University of Kentucky
Washington and Lee University
University of Louisville
Berea College
Transylvania University
Eastern Kentucky University
Lincoln Memorial University